BILINGUAL EDITION
PORTUGUESE ORIGINALS | ENGLISH TRANSLATIONS

CLEPSYDRA
THE POETRY OF CAMILO PESSANHA

Translated by
Jeffrey Childs

Textual Edition by
Paulo Franchetti

Illustrations by
André Carrilho

Introduction by
Helena Carvalhão Buescu

lisbon
poets
& co.

CLEPSYDRA
THE POETRY OF CAMILO PESSANHA

Translated by
Jeffrey Childs

Textual Edition by
Paulo Franchetti

Illustrations by
André Carrilho

Introduction by
Helena Carvalhão Buescu

lisbon
poets
& co.

TITLE
Clepsydra, The Poetry of Camilo Pessanha

ORIGINAL POEMS IN PORTUGUESE
Camilo Pessanha

ENGLISH TRANSLATIONS
(EXCLUDING INTRODUCTION)
Jeffrey Childs

TEXTUAL EDITION AND NOTE ON THE ORGANIZATION
Paulo Franchetti

INTRODUCTION AND TRANSLATION REVISION
Helena Carvalhão Buescu

ILLUSTRATIONS
André Carrilho

GRAPHIC DESIGN
Dania Afonso (graphic concept)
João Jesus

FONTS
Sabon, originally created by Jan Tschichold | Usual, by Rui Abreu | Cantata One, by Joana Correia

CONCEPT
João Pedro Ruivo
Miguel Neto

EDITORIAL COORDINATION
Miguel Neto

PUBLISHER: Lisbon Poets & Co.
info@lisbonpoets.co

1st edition: Julho 2018, by Multitipo – Artes Gráficas
Lisbon, Portugal

©2018 In a Poem, Lda.
All rights reserved. No part of this publication may be reproduced in any form or by any means without the prior permission of In a Poem, Lda..

ISBN: 978-989-99422-8-8
Legal deposit no. 444549/18

CONTENTS

11	INTRODUCTION
21	PUBLISHER´S NOTE
25	NOTE ON THE ORGANIZATION OF THIS EDITION
31	CONTRIBUTORS
32	BIOGRAPHY OF CAMILO PESSANHA

35   CLEPSYDRA

36   *Eu vi a luz em um país perdido*
        I saw the light in a country now gone by

40   Violoncelo
        Violoncello

44   *Na cadeia os bandidos presos!*
        The bandits are locked up in prison!

46   *Depois da luta e depois da conquista*
        After the struggle and after the conquest

48   *Se andava no jardim*
        If she wandered in the garden

50   *Voz débil que passas*
        Fragile voice that undergoes

54   Paisagens de Inverno
        Winter Landscapes

54   I. *Ó meu coração, torna para trás*
            I. O my heart, I beseech you to return

56   II. *Passou o outono já, já torna o frio...*
            II. Autumn has passed, and now the cold returns...

58   I. *Desce em folhedos tenros a colina*
            I. Descend the hill among tender foliage

60   II. *Esvelta surge! Vem das águas, nua*
            II. Lithe, she rises! She steps, naked, from the water

62	Vénus **Venus**
62	I. À flor da vaga, o seu cabelo verde **I. Carried on a wave, her green hair flowing**
64	II. Singra o navio. Sob a água clara **II. The ship sails on. Beneath the clear water**
66	Quem poluiu, quem rasgou os meus lençóis de linho **Who soiled these linens, who left them stained and torn**
68	I. Imagens que passais pela retina **I. Images that flicker across the retinas**
70	II. Quando voltei encontrei os meus passos **II. When I returned I found my footsteps**
74	Desejos **Desires**
78	Madrigal **Madrigal**
80	Soneto de Gelo **Ice Sonnet**
82	I. Tenho sonhos cruéis: n'alma doente **I. I have cruel dreams: in my ailing soul**
84	II. Encontraste-me um dia no caminho **II. You found me one day as I walked down the road**
86	III. Fez-nos bem, muito bem, esta demora **III. It did us good, much good, this delay**
88	Crepuscular **Crepuscular**
90	? **?**
92	Estátua **Statue**

94		*Ó Madalena, ó cabelos de rastos* **O Mary Magdalene, O hair in matted strands**
96		*Canção da Partida* **Song of Departure**
100		*Depois das bodas de oiro* **After the golden anniversary**
102		*Meus olhos apagados* **My listless eyes**
104		*Quando se erguerão as seteiras* **When will the crenels rise again**
108		*O meu coração desce* **My heart descends**
110		*I. E eis quanto resta do idílio acabado* **I. Of the finished idyll this is what remains**
112		*II. Floriram por engano as rosas bravas* **II. The wild roses blossomed mistakenly**
114		*Foi um dia de inúteis agonias* **It was a day of useless agonies**
116		*Fonógrafo* **Phonograph**
118		*Vida* **Life**
120		San Gabriel **Saint Gabriel**
120		*I. Inútil! Calmaria. Já colheram* **I. Useless! A lull. They have gathered up**
122		*II. Vem conduzir as naus, as caravelas* **II. Come, the ships and the caravels you must steer**
124		*Viola Chinesa* **Chinese Guitar**

126	Ao Longe os Barcos de Flores **Boats of Flowers in the Distance**
130	A boémia não morreu **Bohemia is still alive**
132	Rosas de Inverno **Winter Roses**
134	Em um Retrato **In a Portrait**
136	Desce enfim sobre o meu coração **It descends at last to cover my heart**
138	Porque o melhor, enfim **Because the best, alas**
144	Rufando apressado **Hurriedly, with lively roll**
146	Tatuagens complicadas do meu peito! **Intricate tattoos displayed upon my chest!**
148	Branco e Vermelho **White and Red**
158	Ó cores virtuais que jazeis subterrâneas **O virtual colors that lie subterranean**
160	**UNFINISHED POEMS, TWO SATIRICAL SONNETS AND FRAGMENTS RECALLED FROM MEMORY BY OTHERS**
163	**UNFINISHED POEMS**
164	Enfim, levantou ferro **At last the anchor was raised**
168	Cristalizações salinas **Saline crystallizations**

170	*Só o meu crânio fique* **My skull alone does yet reside**
172	*Nesgas agudas do areal* **Jagged fingers of the sands**
175	**TWO SATIRICAL SONNETS**
176	*I. (ou II.) A Miragem* **I. (or II.) The Mirage**
178	*II. (ou I.) Transfiguração* **II. (or I.) Transfiguration**
181	**FRAGMENTS RECALLED FROM MEMORY BY OTHERS**
182	*Ó Terra doce e boa* **O Terra, sweet and good**
184	*Um fio a desdobar, que não termina* **A thread unfolding, never ending**
186	**BRIEF BIBLIOGRAPHY**

INTRODUCTION

HUMAN, ALL TOO HUMAN
THE POETRY OF CAMILO PESSANHA

Nietzsche's book of aphorisms, *Human, all too human. A book for free spirits*, first published between 1878 and 1880, may well be considered an apt fore-description of Camilo Pessanha as a poet – and as a human being.

Camilo Pessanha's biography is well known, and I will just recall here some of the main episodes and dates that converge into the key idea that I want to make: his "free-spiritedness", as well as the suffering that inevitably comes with it.

Born in Coimbra in 1867, Pessanha lived and worked in Macau from 1894 until his death, from excessive opium consumption, in 1926, having meanwhile returned to Portugal for visits due to his faltering health. During these visits, he always contacted his good friend and intellectual Ana de Castro Osório, who was responsible for the publication of Pessanha's only poetry book in 1920, *Clepsydra*. Before and after that, his poems appeared in different periodicals, like *Centauro*, (where he published 16 poems in a row, in 1916), *O Progresso*, or *Novidades*, among others. Some of his poems were only published after his death. A rigorous and detailed description of the critical and genetic dilemmas in the publication of Pessanha's work can be found in this volume, written by one of the critics who has for many years devoted his attention to *Clepsydra* and the rest of Camilo Pessanha's work, Paulo Franchetti. Suffice it to say that distance and undoubtedly his own temperament, and probably his own idea of what poetry and a poet may be, combined to render Pessanha's poetry a critical problem, which has, however, gradually approached an acceptable solution, as in the current edition.

Nietzsche's aphorism on the "human, all too-human" appears in fragment 35 of his eponymous book – and it is not difficult to understand why it is the expression chosen by the author as the title for the book as a whole. After all, the "free spirit" (who will evolve afterwards in Nietzsche's thinking) is the one who assembles in himself all that belongs to humanity (or refined consciousness) itself, and therefore concentrates the awareness of incompleteness, of forgetting, of a sense of life in which most probably sense has altogether disappeared. This human quality is the awareness of inhumanity itself. Pessanha, who is generally associated (and rightly so) with symbolism, through the imagery used and the symbols that he proposes as a metaphorical reading of the world and its sensations, may from a different perspective also be considered distanced from it. Actually, the reader becomes aware of an underlying allegorical narrative, which may bring his poetry into the realm of modernism itself, as it conceives of human existence as a process of depersonalization. In Portuguese poetry, Pessanha's connections with modernist poets such as Mário de Sá-Carneiro (1890-1916) and Fernando Pessoa (1888-1935) are absolutely central, and his poetry enlightens much of these poets' production.

However, what is rendered in (some) Mário de Sá-Carneiro and (some) Pessoa as a kind of frenzied dynamism connected for instance to war, and to the inception of futurism, dadaism or surrealism, becomes in Pessanha a description of apathy, as the image of the eternal deception and delusion, from which there is no escape. Winter roses bloom out of time ("Floriram por engano as rosas bravas"); the medieval imagery is brought forward only to show its inner void and anachronism ("Quando se erguerão as seteiras"); deleted epitaphs are there as a confirmation that names and human beings may never be brought to memory (less even to life) ("E eis quanto resta do idílio acabado"); ships with the yellow flag of plague cross the oceans ("Enfim, levantou ferro"); footsteps in the sand will inevitably disappear ("Quando voltei encontrei os meus passos").

The absence of any action – better: the absence of any possibility of action, other than a symbolic one, becomes a substantiation of the hollowness of life itself, of history, of long-lived traditions: the Discoveries ("San Gabriel"); Shakespeare (with Ophelia as Venus decomposing underwater); and even, in several poems but most poignantly in one of the most beautiful sonnets ever written in Portuguese, "Quem poluiu, quem rasgou os meus lençóis de linho", of Christianity itself, with a human-God who will not be able to live or die, and therefore with a humanity who will never be redeemed. For Pessanha, unlike Yeats, there will be no "Second Coming", ever. The sonnet "Transfiguração" represents psalms, requiems sung by the small voices of a still nature (marsh, fen). And the poet's association with Christ will take the form not of a symbolic redemption, but of eternal suffering, which nobody (not even his mother...) can ever redeem. The New Testament and especially the Book of Revelation are revisited, but they offer no consolation whatsoever.

The poet therefore becomes the symbol of an all-too-human figure, fragile or immobile, in sheer contrast with a reality characterized by its fleetingness and cinematic qualities ("Imagens que passais pela retina"), which nothing can fix. This contrast also takes a discursive form, between a philosophical discourse and reflection on suffering and death, on the one hand, and, on the other, a sensorial discourse, particularly attuned to recognize and render the sensorial materiality of taste, sight, touch, smell, and sound – and able to exploit the synaesthesia that emerges from their conflation (as Baudelaire and Rimbaud had done). Suffering is therefore described as an allegorical scenery not far from Baroque metaphysical concreteness, and its unsolved anxieties (see both sonnets of "Paisagens de Inverno", for instance), where sensations such as frigidity, minerality, iciness ("Ice Sonnet"), odour, inconsistency of haze or breath, and visual transience touch the poet without leaving any fixed trace. This is the state about which Nietzsche refers to as "(…) the consequences that lie in that profound suspiciousness, something of the fears and frosts of isolation to which that unconditional *disparity of view* condemns him who is infected with it (…)" (5)[1]. Pessanha partakes of this "unconditional disparity of view" that "condemns" the "free spirit" to "isolation". However, without it, he would never be a "free spirit".

That is also why we may come to view Pessanha's dialogue between fixity and liquidness, the mineral and solid quality of the world and the shadowy fluidity of sensations

---

1. Friedrich Nietzsche, *Human, all too human. A book for free spirits*, ed. Richard Schacht, transl. R. J. Hollingdale, Cambridge UP, 1996.

in the light of that which Nietzsche defines, in his fragment 2 (13), as the awareness that "Everything has become: there are no *eternal facts*, just as there are no absolute truths. Consequently what is needed from now on is historical philosophizing, and with it the virtue of modesty". This does not mean that everything is relative, but that knowledge (or, better, cognition) is intimately linked with perspective, and therefore with the historical thinking of a "free spirit". The link between *historical philosophizing* and the virtue of modesty is also crucial in this respect: it projects and contributes to the view of a human being "all too human", by way of how his modesty (never leaving a trace...) nevertheless connects him intimately with the world.

Camilo Pessanha may thus be considered as an embodiment of this "free spirit", for whom "everything has become". Someone who looks poetically, philosophically, and historically at the world; who describes its sensorial concreteness, both fixed and fluid, through its impressionistic qualities; one who is "modestly" aware of the historical "deletion" ("delido") of matter, whatever its empirical manifestation.

Nietzsche's model, in fragment 35, is La Rochefoucauld and his use of "maxim thinking" to pinpoint the "all-too-human" character of the free spirit. And, when we read Pessanha, it is not difficult to understand how the idea of "maxim thinking" (or its close relatives, like the epitaph, or even the epigraph) underlies all his poetical work: through the power of imaginatively isolating an impressive moment in the course of events, and nonetheless subduing it in the hurried flow of everything material and its "becoming", the poet is, in Pessanha, closely linked with the one who is able to write, however fleetingly, what is otherwise un-writeable. But the poet is also the one who has the modesty to admit it. Pessanha does not belong to that family of poets who Nietzsche describes, in fragment 148, as "alleviators of life" (81). Quite the contrary: he is the perfect scribe of how life (the "burden of life", to use once more a Nietzschean expression) cannot be alleviated, although it might become bearable, as Nietzsche puts it in fragment 151: "Art makes the sight of life bearable by laying over it the veil of unclear thinking" (82). There is a lot to say about this "veil of unclear thinking", which need not be understood as a relapse into a form of undeveloped cognition, on the contrary. By laying still an additional layer over reality, as symbolists (and modernists) do, the poet modestly describes the elaborate and ultimately unachievable task of being a free spirit in the world, of being all-too-human in the midst of human beings. We may see this in Pessanha's use of form (metrification and, once more, the all-pervading sonnet) as the beautifying labour of art, central to symbolist poetics, and to Pessanha's poetics in particular. His use of formal effects, extremely codified for instance by the balance between stanzas or in his use of meter (the 10-beat line, and its dialogue with other meters); by the radical belatedness of the past, rendered by an imagery mentioned just as a quality of the unattainable; the fleeting characteristic of the present becoming; the contrast between such fluidity and the mineral and solid nature of the world (the sonnet diptych "Venus", and their Ophelian nature); the elusive comprehension of this world by the senses – all make use of an extremely ingenious symbolist poetics that shares with modernism the awareness that poetry (or art) is the possible description of an ontology never of being, but of becoming.

A final note might mark a new beginning, by driving our attention to the title of the only book Pessanha saw published: *Clepsydra*. The use of the anachronism "y" in the word title has several times been noticed, and all critics agree on the fact that such anachronism should (and so is) maintained. But what does it signify? I would suggest that it makes visible the character of "becoming" of reality itself, through an orthography that signals its "awkwardness" and anachronistic quality. But, more than that, it signals the liquid and transient quality of time itself (and, if we accept Zygmunt Bauman's definition, of modernity itself). The crucial characteristic of this description, however, is that it is conveyed by a visual image of both fixity (the object-clepsydra itself) and eternal mobility (the sand or the liquid within it). The first poem of *Clepsydra* is a quatrain, "Eu vi a luz em um país perdido", that is worth quoting in its entirety:

I saw the light in a country now gone by.
My soul is languid and forlorn.
Oh, to slide across the ground without a sigh!
And disappear, like a slithering worm…

Here we have it all, in a poem that serves as a kind of epigraph (and epitaph) to the whole book: a "lost country" that still emits an illusionary light (like some star exploded long ago); a poet that captures this illusion by a motionless soul; life and poetry like modest ways of sliding, leaving no traces, while still "sighing". This quatrain englobes *Clepsydra* as well as the other poems written by Camilo Pessanha and also published in the current volume. A forlorn poetics that takes with it the best of symbolist poetry while re-organizing some of the best characteristics of high modernity itself. It is not only Pessoa who recognizes Camilo Pessanha as one of the poets in the best European tradition – but without him we would not have other contemporary poets such as José Tolentino de Mendonça, Daniel Faria, or Manuel António Pina. Traces are left by those free spirits who live modestly, after all.

This small preface would not be complete without rendering justice to the quality of the translation done by Jeffrey Childs. His reading and translations of Pessanha's poems go back a long way. So do our dialogue about them, our enthusiastic discussions about rhythm, choice of words, syntactic ambiguities, metaphors, and so on. Jeffrey Childs has been a wonderful reader of Pessanha, and he has been able to render into English the elegant, abstract, and sensorial poetry of this poet. His solutions are often surprising for one who has read a line in Portuguese and wondered how its specific quality can reach the same kind of aesthetic effect in English. Childs uses a synthesis of different procedures: he certainly tries to keep rhyme as much as possible, without being imprisoned by it. His awareness of rhythm and its differences in Portuguese and English versification is also very acute, and the solutions found do justice to the sense of musicality that a true symbolist and modernist as Pessanha always tries to achieve. But, besides all this, Jeffrey Childs has a particularly apt semantic capacity for the rendering of Pessanha's images, by keeping their sensorial and simultaneously conceptual connotations. The fact that this particular edition puts together the Portuguese original and the English translation is a wonderful proof of how translation may achieve the rare quality of true poetry itself.

Helena Carvalhão Buescu
Centro de Estudos Comparatistas
Universidade de Lisboa

PUBLISHER'S NOTE

With this volume, we extend the project off divulging the great Portuguese poets in other languages to the publication of an author who, while certainly not a lesser poet, has been – for reasons owing to the course of his life and, perhaps, also to the "veiled" nature of his poetry – less frequently published and less well known among subsequent generations of readers. In fact, far from being considered a forgotten poet – note, for instance, his inclusion in the major anthologies of Portuguese poetry and, in 2017, the commemoration of the 150th anniversary of his birth – Camilo Pessanha has nonetheless always been a poet at the margins.

Born in Coimbra in 1867, Pessanha left for Macau in 1894, first to teach philosophy and later to practice law, becoming a magistrate and holding the position of Administrator of the Land Registry Office. He returned to Portugal only a few times before his death in 1926. Despite his distance to the Portuguese literary milieu of the time, his poems – a few published in journals and newspapers, but most circulated in handwritten form and read or recited in cafés by certain members of the cultural elite of the time – had a strong influence on the first wave of poets of what is now called Portuguese Modernism.

Proof of this enormous influence is Fernando Pessoa's intention, announced in the form of a letter, to publish the poet's work - "a constant source of aesthetic exaltation," with lines of several poems known "by heart" – "in a place of honor" in the third and ill-fated number of the avant-garde journal of the period, *Orpheu*.

But it was not just Pessoa who considered him a "Master," and made clear the importance of Pessanha for that remarkable generation of writers. In response to a query regarding "The most beautiful book of the last 30 years," published in the *República* newspaper in 1914, the poet Mário de Sá-Carneiro wrote perhaps the most beautiful lines ever written about the author of "The wild roses blossomed mistakenly" ("Floriram por engano as rosas bravas"):

> "To my emotional vibration, the best work of Art written in the last thirty years (since Art is fashioned for the nerves to make it vibrate and not for the intellect to measure its lucidity) is a book that has never been published – namely that imperial work that would gather together the unpublished poems of Camilo Pessanha, the great rhythmicist. Hearing his poems for the first time, I was struck by undoubtedly one of the greatest impressions – more intense when of Gold and glorious in their Soul – of my desire to become an Artist. Whirlwinds of New, cumuli of Subtlety, his poems are the settings for magical jewels that change color and melody, arranging them into the rhythms of incantations – mysterious cadences, mirages of Leonines, oscillating obscurities, a rainbow's uncertainties. Heraldic pomp, the shadow of crystal rubbing zebra-like against satin."

This was the book about which Mário de Sá-Carneiro spoke – or an approximation of it – which, in 1920, finally reached publication through the hand of the intellectual, friend and admirer of Camilo Pessanha, Ana de Castro Osório. Under the suggestive title *Clepsydra*, this volume was the only collection of the author's poetry to be published in his lifetime, later suffering considerable additions and alterations at the hand of the publisher's son, João de Castro Osório, in three subsequent editions.

Independently of the controversy that has surrounded these four versions of *Clepsydra*, relative to their different organizational approaches, what is certain is that the editorial impetus behind them – above all the initial one of Ana de Castro Osório – was essential to the dissemination and perpetuation of Camilo Pessanha's poetic work.

It is precisely with the aim of continuing to divulge Pessanha's poetry that the editors conceived of publishing this bilingual edition, which collects under the iconic title, *Clepsydra*, all of the known poetry by Camilo Pessanha, translated in its entirety for the first time into English, with a new organization by one of Pessanha's most renowned scholars, Paulo Franchetti.

To Franchetti we offer our thanks for his dedication and research; to Jeffrey Childs for the care given to the translation of the poetry; to André Carrilho for the artistic vision behind the illustrations; and to Helena Buescu for the thought-provoking introduction, the careful revision and the support provided since the beginning of the project. We thank all of the above for accepting our invitation.

Readers of English (and Portuguese) can thus now enjoy, in a novel format, a work that is today regarded unanimously as one of the crowning achievements of Portuguese lyric poetry.

M.N. / J.P.R.

NOTE ON THE ORGANIZATION OF THIS EDITION

The history and form of the book that collects the poems of Camilo Pessanha has always prompted debate and controversy.

During the poet's last stay in Portugal, in 1915-16, Ana Osório de Castro, his friend and the sister of his close friend Alberto Osório de Castro, asked him to write down or dictate his poems so that they might be gathered together in a volume. The poet did just this, noting in his manuscripts that he had transcribed them "from memory" and correcting the records of his dictations. He had agreed to send additional poems upon his return to Macau – where he kept a notebook of his poems which he would continue to revise until marking them with the word "clean," which indicated his satisfaction with the form achieved[1]. However, additional poems were never sent. Perhaps for this reason, Pessanha's first publisher was prudent in ascribing authorship to the book in a particular way. To note, on the cover of the book did not appear, as convention would suggest, the name of the author at the top and the title of the volume in the middle. The space normally assigned to the name of the author was left blank and the title appeared as *Clepsydra – Poemas de Camilo Pessanha* indicating (as with the case of another important work that emerged from the similar conditions of authorship and coauthorship, *O Livro de Cesário Verde*) its character as a collection done to preserve the poet's work for posterity.

---

1. Pessanha's notebook, which can be consulted in Macau, is reproduced with excellent graphic quality in *Revista de Cultura de Macau*, nos. 11-12 (July-Dec., 1990).

The *Clepsydra* of 1920 is not an edition sanctioned by the author. And João de Castro Osório, Ana de Castro Osório's son, acknowledges this fact when, in 1945 and 1969, after his mother's death, he republished the book and added to the original material many poems that could not have been included in the first edition or whose existence at that time had been unknown.

Additionally, there are clear indications for the sequencing of groupings in the manuscripts that formed the basis of the first edition that were not respected at the time. Such is the case with the sonnets "Images that flicker..." ("Imagens que passais..."), which should have been paired with "When I returned..." ("Quando voltei..."); "Descend the hill..." ("Desce em folhedos..."), which should have been followed by "Lithe, she rises..." ("Esvelta surge..."); and "Of the finished idyll..." ("E eis quanto resta..."), which should have been the first in a pairing that includes "The wild roses blossomed..." ("Floriram por engano..."). Pessanha used numbered markings for these in his manuscripts and, to avoid confusion, took care to identify the pairings referred to, using for this purpose, respectively, one or two asterisks arranged horizontally and two asterisks arranged vertically.

The poet also left indications as to what should be included in his book: a numbered list, discovered in the last years of the 1980s, which was unfortunately only partially preserved. From this list an immediate conclusion can be drawn: Pessanha did not envision the organization of the book in two parts, one for sonnets and another for free-form poetry, this division most certainly belonging to Ana de Castro Osório.

To note:

VIII	Chorae arcadas
IX	Na cadeia os bandidos presos
X	Depois da lucta e depois da conquista
XI	Se andava no jardim +
XII	Voz debil que passas
XIII	Passou o outomno já, já torna o frio +
XIV	Desce em folhêdos tenros a colina +
XV	Singra o navio. Sob a agua clara +
XVI	Quem polluiu, quem rasgou os meus lençoes de linho +
XVII	Imagens que passaes pela retina +

When preparing a critical edition of Pessanha's poetry, I discovered this list among the author's literary remains at the Biblioteca Nacional in Lisbon. It was written on the back of a document (an authorization letter in verse) stuck to the back cover of the volume of *Clepsydra* that had belonged to Ana de Castro Osório. I did not dare detach the document and thus could not understand the symbols (+) after each poem. Over time the sheet came unstuck and the markings made visible. They were observed by the researcher and editor of the site *camilopessanha.com.sapo.pt*, Illídio J. B. Vasco, who communicated their existence to me.

This is an important discovery, since it tells us which sonnets corresponded to the items XIII, XIV, XV and XVII – which form the diptychs for the editions of Pessanha's poetry

I produced for Relógio d'Água (1995) and Ateliê Editorial (2009), in addition to this one. Unfortunately, however, we were unable to determine which poems to pair with items XI and XVI.

An analysis of the document now accessible also allows us to conclude that Pessanha first wrote the verse dedication/authorization to Ana de Castro Osório on the bottom third of a sheet of paper. Then, on the back of the sheet, he ordered the poems in a sequence indicated using Roman numerals. Running out of space there, the list continued on the obverse side. There are still markings that allow us to see that right above the dedication came the poem number XXV and, immediately afterwards, the poem number XXVI. Given the approximate size of the sheet, revealed by the position of the cut in relation to the sequence on the back, the list must have included about 30 lines, which is the number of poems in the first edition, but the numbering of the texts went beyond 30, as indicated by the additions marked with the symbol +.

Although the handwriting of the list reveals some unusual characteristics, it is in all likelihood Pessanha's own, his handwriting being known to vary even within the same page, or line, of writing. In addition to the general similarity to his writing, another factor that supports this idea is that the handwriting is most definitely not that of Ana de Castro Osório, nor that of João or Alberto Osório de Castro; and it seems unreasonable to assume, given the level of respect and admiration surrounding the poet in his friend's home, that anyone there would use the dedication sheet as scrap paper for annotations, even if these were dictated by Pessanha himself.

In this edition, unlike previous ones, Camilo Pessanha's poems are arranged in the following manner: the general body of work is framed by the poem that traditionally opens all editions of *Clepsydra* and the poem the poet indicated, in a manuscript offered to a friend, should be the last of the book. Between these come, first, the poems indicated on what was left of the list described above, followed by the poems that should be grouped with these (as determined by the marking +); afterwards are included all the other poems in the sequence provided by their first public appearance in a periodical or manuscript, according to the research described in the Relógio d'Água edition already mentioned – which does not coincide with a chronological ordering by date of composition, as this is impossible to determine with any precision. Finally, there are some unfinished poems, recorded in manuscripts, two fragments of poems recalled and transcribed from memory by others, and two satirical sonnets.

One final observation: the text of the poems in this edition follows that of the 2009 Brazilian edition, which introduces several important changes with respect to the 1995 Portuguese edition in light of new documents that have arisen through further research, namely the discovery, in Macau, of a copy of the magazine *Centauro* that belonged to Camilo Pessanha and contained several handwritten annotations by the poet.

Paulo Franchetti
Universidade Estadual de Campinas (Brasil)

CONTRIBUTORS

André Carrilho is a designer, illustrator, cartoonist, animator and caricature artist, born in Lisbon, Portugal. He has won several national and international prizes and has shown his work in group and solo exhibitions in Brazil, China, the Czech Republic, France, Portugal, Spain and the USA. In 2002 he was awarded the Gold Award for Illustrator's Portfolio by the Society for News Design (USA), one of the most prestigious illustration awards in the world. His work has been published by *The New York Times*, *The New Yorker*, *Vanity Fair*, *New York Magazine*, *Standpoint*, *Independent on Sunday*, *NZZ am Sonntag*, *Word Magazine*, *Harper's Magazine* and *Diário de Notícias*, among other publications.
www.andrecarrilho.com

Helena Buescu is Professor of Comparative Literature at Universidade de Lisboa. She is a Visiting Professor at universities in Europe, the US, Brazil, and Macau. She has published in Portuguese and international periodicals and books. She is founder-director of the Centre of Comp. Studies (ULisboa) and served on several international boards: ICLA, HERMES, Synapsis, INCH, Inst. World Literature. She serves on European evaluation committees and is a member of Academia Europaea, St. John's College (UCambridge), and Academia das Ciências de Lisboa.

Jeffrey Childs is currently an Assistant Professor of English and American Studies at Universidade Aberta and a researcher at the Center for Comparative Studies and at the Centre for English Studies at the Universidade de Lisboa. He has published translations of several Portuguese-language poets, including Margarida Vale de Gato, Pedro Tamen, Mia Couto, and Manuel Alegre.

Paulo Franchetti is Professor of Literature at Universidade Estadual de Campinas (Brazil). In Brazil, among other works, he has published *Nostalgia, exílio e melancolia - leituras de Camilo Pessanha* and *Estudos de literatura brasileira e portuguesa*. In Portugal, he has published a critical edition of *Clepsydra*, by Camilo Pessanha (Relógio d'Água, 1995), the anthology *As aves que aqui gorjeiam - a poesia do Romantismo ao Simbolismo* (Cotovia, 2005) and the essay *O essencial sobre Camilo Pessanha* (Imprensa Nacional - Casa da Moeda, 2008).

Camilo Pessanha

was born in Coimbra on 7 September 1867. Little is known of his childhood or adolescence. In 1884, he enrolled to study law at the Universidade de Coimbra (University of Coimbra), receiving his degree in June of 1891.

In the middle of 1893, having trouble finding employment in Portugal, Pessanha applied for a teaching position at the recently established Liceu de Macau (Macau Secondary School). The following year he left for China, which would be his home until his death in 1926.

During the time he lived in Portugal, Camilo Pessanha seems to have written little poetry. Yet his first five years in Macau would be the most productive of his life, as it was during this time that he composed roughly half of the poems that we have today. During the four decades he spent in China, Pessanha returned to Portugal on leave several times. His poems, then distributed in manuscript form – as well as in copies of these – circulated among the younger generation of poets and had a significant influence on such poets as Fernando Pessoa and Mário de Sá-Carneiro.

During his last visit to Portugal, in 1915-1916, at the request of Ana de Castro Osório, the poet recorded a list of poems to be gathered in book form and agreed to send along definite versions of these and others – which he never did. Thus, in 1920, Ana de Castro Osório organised and published, using what materials she had, Pessanha's only book: *Clepsydra*.

Absorbed in his studies of Chinese language and art, of which he was a collector, the poet did not return to Portugal. He thus had neither the opportunity nor the time to realize that his work, however slim, would come to be regarded unanimously as one of the crowning achievements of Portuguese lyric poetry.

Clepsydra

Eu vi a luz em um país perdido.
A minha alma é lânguida e inerme.
Oh! Quem pudesse deslizar sem ruído!
No chão sumir-se, como faz um verme...

I saw the light in a country now gone by.
My soul is languid and forlorn.
Oh, to slide across the ground without a sigh!
And disappear, like a slithering worm...

Violoncelo

a Carlos Amaro

    Chorai, arcadas
Do violoncelo,
Convulsionadas.
Pontes aladas
De pesadelo...

    De que esvoaçam,
Brancos, os arcos.
Por baixo passam,
Se despedaçam,
No rio os barcos.

    Fundas, soluçam
Caudais de choro.
Que ruínas, ouçam...
Se se debruçam,
Que sorvedouro!

Violoncello

for Carlos Amaro

    Weep, bowstrings
Of the violoncello,
Convulsing air.
Soaring bridges
Of nightmare…

    Upon which quiver,
White, the arches.
Beneath them, in the river,
The boats pass by
And come undone.

    Deep, the strings release
Torrents of grief.
What ruins, listen…
If they should strain,
A flood through a drain!

Lívidos astros,
Soidões lacustres...
Lemes e mastros...
E os alabastros
Dos balaústres!

Urnas quebradas.
Blocos de gelo!
Chorai, arcadas
Do violoncelo,
Despedaçadas...

Flickering stars,
Lakes of solitude...
Helms and masts...
And the alabaster
Of the balusters!

Broken urns.
Blocks of ice!
Weep, bowstrings
Of the violoncello,
Broken into lesser things...

Na cadeia os bandidos presos!
O seu ar de contemplativos!
Que é das feras de olhos acesos?...
Pobres de seus olhos cativos...

Passeiam mudos entre as grades.
Parecem peixes num aquário.
Campo florido das saudades,
Porque rebentas tumultuário?

Serenos. Serenos. Serenos.
Trouxe-os algemados a escolta...
Estranha taça de venenos,
Meu coração sempre em revolta!

Coração, quietinho, quietinho!
Porque te insurges e blasfemas?

Pss... Não batas... Devagarinho...
Olha os soldados, as algemas.

The bandits are locked up in prison!
Their air is quiet and contemplative!
What of the wild beasts with burning eyes?...
The poverty of eyes held captive...

They pace silently behind the bars,
Resembling fish in an aquarium.
Field flowering with anguished longing,
Why erupt in pandemonium?

Serene. Serene. Serene.
They are escorted about in chains...
What a strange tumbler of poison,
My heart in constant rebellion!

Be quiet, my heart, be quiet!
Why rise up in blasphemous riot?

Shhh... Go slowly... Without a fight...
Note the soldiers, how the shackles bite.

Depois da luta e depois da conquista
Fiquei só! Fora um acto antipático!
Deserta a Ilha, e no lençol aquático
Tudo verde, verde, – a perder de vista.

Porque vos fostes, minhas caravelas,
Carregadas de todo o meu tesoiro?
– Longas teias de luar de lhama de oiro,
Legendas a diamantes das estrelas!

Quem vos desfez, formas inconsistentes,
Por cujo amor escalei a muralha,
– Leão armado, uma espada nos dentes?

Felizes vós, ó mortos da batalha!
Sonhais, de costas, nos olhos abertos
Reflectindo as estrelas, boquiabertos...

After the struggle and after the conquest
I remained alone! How reckless such an act!
Deserted Isle that lies on a watery plain
Green, all green – nor else until the eyes arrest.

Oh why, my caravels, tell me why
Did you depart, bearing all my treasure?
– Long moonlit webs of golden llama,
Keys to the diamonds gleaming in the sky!

Who undid you, you of inconsistent shape,
For whose love I scaled the castle wall,
– A lion armed, sword clenched between my teeth?

Happy are you who did in battle fall!
You dream, on your backs, reflecting the stars
In eyes wide open, with your mouths agape…

Se andava no jardim,
Que cheiro de jasmim!
Tão branca do luar!

....
....
....

Eis tenho-a junto a mim.
Vencida, é minha, enfim,
Após tanto a sonhar...

Porque entristeço assim?...
Não era ela, mas sim
(O que eu quis abraçar),

A hora do jardim...
O aroma de jasmim...
A onda do luar...

If she wandered in the garden
What a scent of jasmine!
How white in the moonlight!

      ….
….
….

Now I have her at my side.
Alas, defeated, she is mine,
Having so long been my dream…

Why, then, do I sadden thus?…
It wasn't her, but something else
(That I wanted to hold tight),

The hour of the garden…
The scent of the jasmine…
The beam of moonlight…

Voz débil que passas,
Que humílima gemes
Não sei que desgraças...

Dir-se-ia que pedes.
Dir-se-ia que tremes,
Unida às paredes,

Se vens, às escuras,
Confiar-me ao ouvido
Não sei que amarguras...

Suspiras ou falas?
Porque é o gemido,
O sopro que exalas?

Dir-se-ia que rezas.
Murmuras baixinho
Não sei que tristezas...

– Ser teu companheiro? –
Não sei o caminho.
Eu sou estrangeiro.

    Fragile voice that undergoes,
That meekly murmurs
Unimagined woes…

    One would say you seem to call.
One would say you tremble,
Your back against the wall,

    If you come, in the darkness,
To whisper in my ear
Unimagined bitterness…

    Do you sigh or do you speak?
Why is there a murmur
In the breath that you expire?

    You appear to pray.
Mumbling softly
What sorrows I cannot say…

    – To walk with you hand in hand? –
I do not know the way.
I am foreign to this land.

– Passados amores? –
Animas-te, dizes
Não sei que terrores…

Fraquinha, deliras.
– Projectos felizes? –
Suspiras. Expiras.

– What of loves foregone? –
Cheer up, you say
What fears must linger on…

You grow delirious as you tire.
– Visions of happiness? –
You murmur. You expire.

Paisagens de Inverno

I
a Alberto Osório de Castro

Ó meu coração, torna para trás.
Onde vais a correr desatinado?
Meus olhos incendidos que o pecado
Queimou! Volvei, longas noites de paz.

Vergam da neve os olmos dos caminhos.
A cinza arrefeceu sobre o brasido.
Noites da serra, o casebre transido...
Cismai, meus olhos, como uns velhinhos.

Extintas primaveras, evocai-as.
Já vai florir o pomar das macieiras.
Hemos de enfeitar os chapéus de maias.

Sossegai, esfriai, olhos febris...
Hemos de ir a cantar nas derradeiras
Ladainhas... Doces vozes senis.

Winter Landscapes

I

for Alberto Osório de Castro

O my heart, I beseech you to return.
Where do you run so impulsive and headlong?
My eyes, with sin, were set ablaze
And burned! For nights of peace restored I yearn.

The elms that line the paths are bent with snow.
The once fiery coals have cooled to ash.
Nights spent in the mountains, a hut trespassed…
Brood, my eyes, the way that old men know.

Springtimes long extinct, summon them forth:
Soon the apple trees will be in bloom.
And we shall decorate our hats with broom.

Settle down, cool down, my feverish eyes…
For we shall go and sing the final
Litanies… Voices delicate and senile.

II
a Abel Annibal de Azevedo

    Passou o outono já, já torna o frio...
– Outono de seu riso magoado.
Álgido inverno! Oblíquo o sol, gelado...
– O sol, e as águas límpidas do rio.

    Águas claras do rio! Águas do rio,
Fugindo sob o meu olhar cansado,
Para onde me levais meu vão cuidado?
Aonde vais, meu coração vazio?
    Ficai, cabelos dela, flutuando,
E, debaixo das águas fugidias,
Os seus olhos abertos e cismando...

    Onde ides a correr, melancolias?
– E, refractadas, longamente ondeando,
As suas mãos translúcidas e frias...

II
for Abel Annibal de Azevedo

    Autumn has passed, and now the cold returns…
– Autumn with its damaged smile.
Frigid winter! Oblique, the frozen sun…
– The sun, and the limpid waters of the river.

    Clear waters of the river! Waters of the river,
From my tired gaze never ceasing to depart,
Where are you taking my vain attention?
Where are you going, my empty heart?

    Her flowing tresses remain there floating,
And, just beneath the fleeting waters,
Her eyes are open, wondering and bold…

    Where are you running to, O melancholy?
– And refracted, undulating slowly,
Are her hands, translucent and cold…

I
a José Pessanha

Desce em folhedos tenros a colina:
– Em glaucos, frouxos tons adormecidos,
Que saram, frescos, meus olhos ardidos,
Nos quais a chama do furor declina...

Oh vem, de branco, – do imo da folhagem!
Os ramos, leve, a tua mão aparte.
Oh vem! Meus olhos querem desposar-te,
Reflectir-te virgem a serena imagem.

De silva doida uma haste esquiva
Quão delicada te osculou num dedo
Com um aljôfar cor-de-rosa viva!...

Ligeira a saia... Doce brisa, impele-a.
Oh vem! De branco! Do imo do arvoredo!
Alma de silfo, carne de camélia...

I
for José Pessanha

 Descend the hill among tender foliage:
– In glaucous, in weak sleeping tones,
Whose freshness soothes my burning eyes,
In which the flame of fervor lessens…

 Oh come, in white – from the depths of foliage!
The branches your hand so lightly sweeps away.
Oh come! The one my eyes seek to espouse,
Reflecting, virgin, your serene image.

 From a frenzied bramble a wayward branch
So delicately caressed your finger
Drawing a pink droplet of living dew!…

 So slight the skirt… Sweet breeze, give it a tug…
Oh come! In white! From the depths of the silva!
Soul of a sylph and flesh of a camellia…

II

    Esvelta surge! Vem das águas, nua,
Timonando uma concha alvinitente!
Os rins flexíveis e o seio fremente...
Morre-me a boca por beijar a tua.

    Sem vil pudor! Do que há que ter vergonha?
Eis-me formoso, moço e casto, forte.
Tão branco o peito! – para o expor à Morte...
Mas que ora – a infame! – não se te anteponha.

    A hidra torpe!... Que a estrangulo... Esmago-a
De encontro à rocha onde a cabeça te há-de,
Com os cabelos escorrendo água,

    Ir inclinar-se, desmaiar de amor,
Sob o fervor da minha virgindade
E o meu pulso de jovem gladiador.

II

    Lithe, she rises! She steps, naked, from the water,
Turning a white conch like the helm of a ship!
Her hips are supple and bosom aflutter...
My mouth hungers for the touch of your lip.

    Without vile modesty! What reason for remorse?
Here I stand: young, handsome, chaste, and strong.
With a chest so white! – to display to Death...
Keep vile death, for now, unwitting of your course.

    The base hydra!... Which I smother... Crushing it
Against the rock where, one day, your head will,
With water streaming freely from your hair,

    Tilt upward, swooning in love's exalted air,
Beneath my virginity's ardent fervor,
In the firm embrace of a young gladiator.

Vénus

a Pires Avellanoso

I

À flor da vaga, o seu cabelo verde,
Que o torvelinho enreda e desenreda...
O cheiro a carne que nos embebeda!
Em que desvios a razão se perde!

Pútrido o ventre, azul e aglutinoso,
Que a onda, crassa, num balanço alaga,
E reflui (um olfacto que se embriaga)
Como em um sorvo, múrmura de gozo.

O seu esboço, na marinha turva...
De pé, flutua, levemente curva,
Ficam-lhe os pés atrás, como voando...

E as ondas lutam como feras mugem,
A lia em que a desfazem disputando,
E arrastando-a na areia, co'a salsugem.

Venus

for Pires Avellanoso

I

    Carried on a wave, her green hair flowing,
Which this swirling tangles and untangles…
The scent of flesh is intoxicating!
And reason is lost in countless eddies!

    Putrid the womb, blue and glutinous,
That the turbid wave rolls in to flood,
And flows back (a scent inebrious)
As in a draught, a murmur of pleasure.

    Her outline, in the cloudy reflux…
Upright, floating, a forward bend so slight,
Her feet behind her, as if she were in flight…

    And the waves struggle as wild beasts whine,
Rending her into sludge as they fight,
And dragging her up the sand with the brine.

II

Singra o navio. Sob a água clara
Vê-se o fundo do mar, de areia fina...
Impecável figura peregrina,
A distância sem fim que nos separa!

Seixinhos da mais alva porcelana,
Conchinhas tenuemente cor-de-rosa,
Na fria transparência luminosa
Repousam, fundos, sob a água plana.

E a vista sonda, reconstrui, compara.
Tantos naufrágios, perdições, destroços!
Ó fúlgida visão, linda mentira!

Róseas unhinhas que a maré partira...
Dentinhos que o vaivém desengastara...
Conchas, pedrinhas, pedacinhos de ossos...

II

    The ship sails on. Beneath the clear water
The fine sand of the ocean floor can be seen...
Impeccable wayfaring figure,
The limitless distance that lies between!

    Little fragments of the whitest porcelain,
Small seashells of the most delicate rose,
In the cold luminous transparency,
Deep under the water's surface, they repose.

    And sight begins to plumb, rebuild, compare.
So many shipwrecks, so much ruin and loss!
O dazzling vision, O lie so fair!

    Roseate fingernails the tide has broken...
Teeth the ebb and flow has worn away...
Bits of shell, stone and bone awash in the fray...

Quem poluiu, quem rasgou os meus lençóis de linho,
Onde esperei morrer, – meus tão castos lençóis?
Do meu jardim exíguo os altos girassóis
Quem foi que os arrancou e lançou ao caminho?

Quem quebrou (que furor cruel e simiesco!)
A mesa de eu cear, – tábua tosca, de pinho?
E me espalhou a lenha? E me entornou o vinho?
– Da minha vinha o vinho acidulado e fresco...

Ó minha pobre mãe!... Não te ergas mais da cova.
Olha a noite, olha o vento. Em ruína a casa nova...
Dos meus ossos o lume a extinguir-se breve.

Não venhas mais ao lar. Não vagabundes mais,
Alma da minha mãe... Não andes mais à neve,
De noite a mendigar às portas dos casais.

Who soiled these linens, who left them stained and torn,
My sheets – so chaste – in which I'd hoped to die?
The lofty sunflowers in my meagre garden,
Who snatched and strew these where the earth is worn?

Who broke (what cruel and simian fury!)
The table on which I dine, – a slab of rough pine?
And scattered my firewood? And spilled my wine?
– The pungent and refreshing spirits of my vines…

Oh, poor mother!… Rise no longer from the grave.
Look at the night, the wind. The new house in ruins…
Soon the light will be extinguished from my bones.

Do not come home again. Roam about no more,
My mother's soul… Drift no longer through the snow,
Nor at night continue begging door to door.

I

a João Jardim

    Imagens que passais pela retina
Dos meus olhos, porque não vos fixais?
Que passais como a água cristalina
Por uma fonte para nunca mais!...

    Ou para o lago escuro onde termina
Vosso curso, silente de juncais,
E o vago medo angustioso domina,
– Porque ides sem mim, não me levais?

    Sem vós o que são os meus olhos abertos?
– O espelho inútil, meus olhos pagãos!
Aridez de sucessivos desertos...

    Fica sequer, sombra das minhas mãos,
Flexão casual de meus dedos incertos,
– Estranha sombra em movimentos vãos.

I
for João Jardim

     Images that flicker across the retinas
Of my eyes, why is it you do not remain?
You who like the crystalline water
Of a spring flow on into never again!...

     Or into the dark lake that marks the terminus
Of your course, silent among the rushes,
And the vague anguishing fear begins to swell,
– Why leave without me, why not take me as well?

     Without you, what becomes of my open eyes?
– My pagan eyes, naught but a useless mirror!
The dryness of where desert upon desert lies...

     Not even the shadows of my hands remain,
Uncertain fingers flexed in casual repose,
– The strange shadows of movements made in vain.

II
a Ayres de Castro e Almeida

Quando voltei encontrei os meus passos
Ainda frescos sobre a húmida areia.
A fugitiva hora, reevoquei-a,
– Tão rediviva!, nos meus olhos baços...

Olhos turvos de lágrimas contidas.
– Mesquinhos passos, porque doidejastes
Assim transviados, e depois tornastes
Ao ponto das primeiras despedidas?

Onde fostes sem tino, ao vento vário,
Em redor, como as aves num aviário,
Até que a asita fofa lhes faleça...

Toda esta extensa pista – para quê?
Se há-de vir apagar-vos a maré,
Com as do novo rasto que começa...

II
for Ayres de Castro e Almeida

    When I returned I found my footsteps
Still stamped upon the humid sand.
The fugitive hour I then recalled,
– So alive! – within these eyes so dull…

    Eyes grown cloudy with tears held in check.
– Trifling steps, why carry on so far
From some unswerving path, and circle back
To the place of your first valediction?

    Where you went uncouth, blown by any blast,
In circles, like fowl in a hatchery,
Until their downy wings must fail at last…

    All these far-reaching tracks – what can they mean?
If soon the tide rolls in to wipe them clean,
And prime the sand for a new inscription…

Violoncelo

(A Carlos Amaro)

Chora, arcador
De violoncelo,
Comissionado.
Conta a dor
De pesadelo...

De joanesquem,
Bromcos, ox arcos.
Por baixo passam,
Se despedaçam,
Estão os tarcos.

Funcham, soluçam
Cascatas de clavos.
Que ruínas, oh gensos...
Se se debruçam,
Que sonadores!

Lívidos astros,
Sóidios lamentos...
Temas e martírios...
E os alabastros
Dos balaustres!

Photograph of the manuscript that belonged to Carlos Amaro.
Courtesy of Daniel Pires.

This is the most recent manuscript of the poem "Violoncello" ("Violoncelo"), which heads the fragment of the list of texts that compose *Clepsydra*, there pointed by its first verse "Chorae arcadas" (see p. 27). It was sent by the poet to his friend, Carlos Amaro. Considering that there is a record of it being sent from Macau, that it is without additional markings, corrections or the indication "from memory" and that it follows modern spelling (unlike previous versions), there is no doubt that it represents the final known wishes of the author.

Up until this point in the book, the poems have been organized according to the design of the poet. From this page on appear those poems whose position in the book is unknown (if, in fact, they would all have been included) and, for this reason, these are arranged according to their first recorded appearance in published form or dated manuscript.

Desejos

    Se medito no gozo que promete
A sua boca fresca e pequenina
E o seio mergulhado em renda fina,
Sob a curva ligeira do corpete,

    Desejo, nuns transportes de gigante,
Estreitá-la de rijo entre meus braços,
Até quase esmagar nestes abraços
A sua carne branca e palpitante;

    Como, d'Ásia nos bosques tropicais,
Apertam em espiral auriluzente,
Os músculos hercúleos da serpente
Aos troncos das palmeiras colossais...

    E como ao depois, quando o cansaço
A sepulta na morna letargia,
Dormitando repousa todo o dia
À sombra da palmeira o corpo lasso;

Desires

    If I meditate on the promise
Of pleasure made by her mouth, small and fresh,
And her breasts hidden, in elegant lace,
Under the gentle rise of her bodice,

    I desire, in a tremendous rush,
To take her hard between these arms and press
Until I reach the point at which I'd crush
Her white and palpitating flesh;

    As, in Asia's woods, dense and tropical,
The serpent's herculean muscle
Enwraps in a glimmering spiral
The trunks of the colossal palms…

    As weariness, when passions fade away,
Buries in its tepid lethargy
The slack body, which drowses fitfully
In the shade of a palm the rest of the day;

Eu quisera também, adormecido,
Dos fantasmas da febre ver o mar,
Mas sempre sob o azul do seu olhar,
Envolto no calor do seu vestido;

Como os ébrios chineses delirantes
Aspiram, já dormindo, o fumo quieto
Que o seu longo cachimbo predilecto
No ambiente espalhava pouco antes...

Asleep, amidst the ghosts of fever, I too
Had longed to gaze upon the sea, but, alas,
Always under the deep and sultry blue
Of her stare, wrapped in the heat of her dress;

As the Chinese patrons, asleep on the floor,
wasted and dazed, inhale the quiet smoke
Blown through their long and treasured pipe
Into the cloud-heavy room moments before…

Madrigal

Aquela enorme frieza
Não entristeça ninguém...
Ela estende o seu desdém
À sua própria beleza:

Quando, solta do vestido,
Sai da frescura do banho,
O seu cabelo castanho,
Esse cabelo comprido,

Que frio, que desconsolo!
Deixa ficar-se pendente,
Em vez de feito em serpente
Ir enroscar-se-lhe ao colo!

Madrigal

    That overwhelming coldness
Should sadness bring to none…
She casts upon her beauty
A disdain that's all her own:

    When, free of her dress, she steps bare
From the freshness of her bath,
Her dark brown locks,
Those long locks of flowing hair,

    How cold, what mark of despair!
Hang there loose and dangling,
Instead of, snake-like, coiling
Into her bosom so fair!

Soneto de Gelo

Ingénuo sonhador – as crenças d'oiro
Não as vás derruir, deixa o destino
Levar-te no teu berço de bambino,
Porque podes perder esse tesoiro.

Tens na crença um farol. Nem o procuras,
Mas bem o vês luzir sobre o infinito!...
E o homem que pensou, – foi um precito,
Buscando a luz em vão – sempre às escuras.

Eu mesmo quero a fé, e não a tenho,
– Um resto de batel – quisera um lenho,
Para não afundir na treva imensa,

O Deus, o mesmo Deus que te fez crente...
Nem saibas que esse Deus omnipotente
Foi quem arrebatou a minha crença.

Ice Sonnet

    Ingenuous dreamer – those beliefs of gold,
Do not tear them down; let fate unfold
And carry you away in your cradle,
For that is the treasure you stand to lose.

    Your belief is a lighthouse. Without searching,
You watch it cast its light over infinity!...
And the man who thought – condemned, in vain
Searching for the light – will in darkness remain.

    I long for a faith that escapes me somehow...
– The remains of a boat – perhaps a fallen bough
To keep from drowning in the immense darkness,

    The Lord, the same Lord who made you believe...
That God almighty, may you not wonder,
Was He who tore my faith asunder.

I

    Tenho sonhos cruéis: n'alma doente
Sinto um vago receio prematuro.
Vou a medo na aresta do futuro,
Embebido em saudades do presente...

    Saudades desta dor que em vão procuro
Do peito afugentar bem rudemente,
Devendo ao desmaiar sobre o poente,
Cobrir-m'o coração dum véu escuro!...

    Porque a dor, esta falta d'harmonia,
Toda a luz desgrenhada que alumia
As almas doidamente, o céu d'agora,

    Sem ela o coração é quase nada:
– Um sol onde expirasse a madrugada,
Porque é só madrugada quando chora.

I

    I have cruel dreams: in my ailing soul
I feel a disquiet, vague and premature.
I inch meekly along the edge of the future,
Intoxicated by a longing for the present...

    Longing for this affliction I seek in vain
To drive boorishly from my chest,
I must, as the light flickers on the west,
Cover my heart with a dark veil!...

    For pain, this absence of harmony,
All of the tangled rays that madly
Illuminate these souls, the sky of today,

    Without it the heart is next to nothing:
A sun emptied of the dawn of tomorrow
For dawn lives only in the presence of sorrow.

II

Encontraste-me um dia no caminho
Em procura de quê, nem eu o sei.
– Bom dia, companheiro, te saudei,
Que a jornada é maior indo sozinho.

É longe, é muito longe, há muito espinho!
Paraste a repousar, eu descansei...
Na venda em que poisaste, onde poisei,
Bebemos cada um do mesmo vinho.

É no monte escabroso, solitário,
Corta os pés como a rocha dum calvário,
E queima como a areia!... Foi no entanto

Que chorámos a dor de cada um...
E o vinho em que choraste era comum:
Tivemos que beber do mesmo pranto.

II

    You found me one day as I walked down the road
Searching for what I myself cannot say.
I hailed as we met: "My companion, good day!"
A journey is longer when travelled alone.

    It's long, so long, the path littered with thorns!
You stopped for a rest and a rest sounded fine…
In the shop where we stopped and both found a seat,
We each drank in turn from the same cup of wine.

    It was on a hill, barren and solitary,
That cuts one's feet like the rock of Calvary
And scorches like sand!… And yet it was here

    We broke down for what each bore in pain…
And the wine into which you wept was the same:
We each had to drink from the same cup of tears.

III

Fez-nos bem, muito bem, esta demora:
Enrijou a coragem fatigada...
Eis os nossos bordões da caminhada,
Vai já rompendo o sol: vamos embora.

Este vinho, mais virgem do que a aurora,
Tão virgem não o temos na jornada...
Enchamos as cabaças: pela estrada,
Daqui inda este néctar avigora!...

Cada um por seu lado!... Eu vou sozinho,
Eu quero arrostar só todo o caminho,
Eu posso resistir à grande calma!...

Deixai-me chorar mais e beber mais,
Perseguir doidamente os meus ideais,
E ter fé e sonhar – encher a alma.

III

It did us good, much good, this delay:
It hardened our waning courage…
These are the staffs that aid us in walking,
The sun is breaking: let's be on our way.

This wine, more virgin than the dawn,
So virgin we have none for the taking…
Let us fill our gourds: on the road
This nectar will keep invigorating!…

Each on his way!… I'll travel alone,
The whole of the road I wish to make my own,
And in travelling shake off this pervading calm!…

Let me grieve further and drink yet more
And madly pursue the ideal from its hole,
And have faith and dream – to round out the soul.

Crepuscular

Há no ambiente um murmúrio de queixume,
De desejos d'amor, d'ais comprimidos...
Uma ternura esparsa de balidos
Sente-se esmorecer como um perfume.

As madressilvas murcham nos silvados
E o aroma que exalam pelo espaço
Tem delíquios de gozo e de cansaço,
Nervosos, femininos, delicados.

Sentem-se espasmos, agonias d'ave,
Inapreensíveis, mínimas, serenas...

Tenho entre as mãos as tuas mãos pequenas,
O meu olhar no teu olhar suave.

As tuas mãos tão brancas d'anemia,
Os teus olhos tão meigos de tristeza...
É este enlanguescer da natureza,
Este vago sofrer do fim do dia.

Crepuscular

There is in the air a murmuring lament
For the desires of love and long drawn-out sighs...
A dispersed tenderness of bleating
Is felt to dissipate like a fragrant scent.

The honeysuckle wilts in the thicket
And the perfume it exhales into space
Bears deliria of pleasure and fatigue
That are nervous, feminine, delicate.

One feels the spasms, hears a birdlike call,
Inapprehensible, minimal, serene...

I hold in my hands your hands so small,
In my eyes your eyes are gentleness seen.

Your hands appear so anemic and white...
Your eyes rendered so soft with dismay...
It is the languishing of nature,
This vague suffering at the close of day.

?

Não sei se isto é amor. Procuro o teu olhar,
Se alguma dor me fere, em busca dum abrigo;
E apesar disso, crês? nunca pensei num lar
Onde fosses feliz, e eu feliz contigo.

Por ti nunca chorei nenhum ideal desfeito.
E nunca te escrevi nenhuns versos românticos.
Nem depois de acordar te procurei no leito,
Como a esposa sensual do Cântico dos cânticos .

Se é amar-te não sei. Não sei se te idealizo
A tua cor sadia, o teu sorriso terno...
Mas sinto-me sorrir de ver esse sorriso
Que me penetra bem, como este sol de inverno.

Passo contigo a tarde, e sempre sem receio
Da luz crepuscular, que enerva, que provoca.
Eu não demoro o olhar na curva do teu seio
Nem me lembrei jamais de te beijar na boca.

Eu não sei se é amor. Será talvez começo.
Eu não sei que mudança a minha alma pressente...
Amor não sei se o é, mas sei que te estremeço,
Que adoecia talvez de te saber doente.

?

I cannot say if this is love. If pain grips me,
My eyes seek out your own, hoping to find shelter;
In spite of this – would you believe? – I've never dreamed
Of a home where you, and I with you, were happy.

For you I've never mourned a dream as it was breaking
And never written a single romantic line.
Nor vainly searched my bed for you on waking,
Like the desirous woman sung by Solomon.

If this is love I cannot say. Nor if, ideal,
I hold you so: your tender smile, your vibrant glow…
But I feel the smile within me when I see your own
Which reaches to my core, much like this winter sun.

Each afternoon I spend with you, I never fear
The dying light that taunts our spirits and unnerves.
My eyes have never lingered on your bosom's curves
Nor have my lips desired that your own draw near.

I cannot say if this is love. Perhaps a start.
I cannot say what change my soul might glimpse within…
Love I cannot say but, as I sense you trembling,
Know that your affliction would render ill my heart.

Estátua

Cansei-me de tentar o teu segredo:
No teu olhar sem cor, – frio escalpelo, –
O meu olhar quebrei, a debatê-lo,
Como a onda na crista dum rochedo.

Segredo dessa alma, e meu degredo
E minha obsessão! Para bebê-lo,
Fui teu lábio oscular, num pesadelo,
Por noites de pavor, cheio de medo.

E o meu ósculo ardente, alucinado,
Esfriou sobre o mármore correcto
Desse entreaberto lábio gelado...

Desse lábio de mármore, discreto,
Severo como um túmulo fechado,
Sereno como um pélago quieto.

Statue

    I grew weary while searching for your key:
In your colorless eyes – what cold scalpel –
My own eyes foundered, struggling to break free,
As a wave breaks on the crest of a rock.

    Secret of that soul, my place of exile,
And my obsession! To taste it I wed
My lips to yours, in a nightmare of nights
Spent trembling with terror and dread.

    And my burning kiss, feverishly dreamt,
Grew cold against the punctilious marble
Of those frozen lips like a force unspent…

    Of those marble lips, as discreet
And severe as a long-sealed tomb,
As deep and serene as the ocean's womb.

...e lhe regou de lágrimas os pés,
e os enxugava com os cabelos da sua cabeça.
Evangelho de S. Lucas

Ó Madalena, ó cabelos de rastos,
Lírio poluído, branca flor inútil,
Meu coração, velha moeda fútil,
E sem relevo, os caracteres gastos,

De resignar-se torpemente dúctil,
Desespero, nudez de seios castos,
Quem também fosse, ó cabelos de rastos,
Ensanguentado, enxovalhado, inútil,

Dentro do peito, abominável cómico!
Morrer tranquilo, – o fastio da cama.
O redenção do mármore anatómico,

Amargura, nudez de seios castos,
Sangrar, poluir-se, ir de rastos na lama,
Ó Madalena, ó cabelos de rastos!

… and began to wash his feet with tears,
and did wipe them with the hairs of her head.
Gospel According to Luke

    O Mary Magdalene, O hair in matted strands,
A tainted lily, a useless white flower,
My heart, an old coin of its value shorn,
Without relief, and all its markings worn,

    From bowing clumsily to resignation,
Despair, the bareness of a chaste bosom,
Would that one were, O hair in matted strands,
Bloodied, useless, subject to deprecation,

    Inside one's chest, horrid and comical!
To die at peace, – the boredom of a bed.
O redemption of marble anatomical,

    Bitterness, the bareness of a chaste bosom,
To bleed, to taint, to grovel on one's hands,
O Mary Magdalene, O hair in matted strands!

Canção da Partida

    Ao meu coração um peso de ferro
Eu hei-de prender na volta do mar.
Ao meu coração um peso de ferro...
Lançá-lo ao mar.

    Quem vai embarcar, que vai degredado,
As penas do amor não queira levar...
Marujos, erguei o cofre pesado,
Lançai-o ao mar.

    E hei-de mercar um fecho de prata.
O meu coração é o cofre selado.
A sete chaves: tem dentro uma carta...
– A última, de antes do teu noivado.

    A sete chaves, – a carta encantada!
E um lenço bordado... Esse hei-de-o levar.
Que é para o molhar na água salgada
No dia em que enfim deixar de chorar.

Song of Departure

      Around my heart lies an iron weight
I shall fasten upon the sea's return.
Around my heart lies an iron weight…
Cast it into the sea.

      For one who embarks, such penance to bear,
The sufferings of love one must not wear…
Sailors, raise up that heavy coffer,
Cast it into the sea.

      And I shall purchase a lock of silver.
My heart, you see, is the well-sealed coffer.
Locked with seven keys: inside there is a letter…
– The last before word of your betrothal.

      With seven keys – the enchanting letter!
And embroidered scarf… The one I'm sure to keep,
The one I'll douse in the salty water
On the day these eyes no longer weep.

Camilo Pessanha next to the University
Tower in Coimbra, with its historical clock.

Depois das bodas de oiro,
Da hora prometida,
Não sei que mau agoiro
Me enoiteceu a vida...

Temo de regressar...
E mata-me a saudade.
Mas de me recordar
Não sei que dor me invade.

Nem quero prosseguir,
Trilhar novos caminhos,
Meus pobres pés dorir,
Já roxos dos espinhos.

Nem ficar, e morrer:
Perder-te, imagem vaga...
Cessar, não mais te ver,
Como uma luz se apaga.

    After the golden anniversary
Of the promised hour,
I know not what dire augury
Has brought upon this night...

    I dread the thought of return...
And longing assails my brain.
Yet each time I remember
I am wracked with a strange pain.

    I do not wish to push ahead,
To discover paths unworn;
My poor feet are aching,
Raw and bloody from the thorns.

    Nor do I wish to stay and die:
To cease, to lose you from my sight,
To surrender you, vague image,
The way a hand turns off the light.

> *Il pleure dans mon coeur*
> *Comme il pleut sur la ville.*
> Verlaine

Meus olhos apagados,
Vede a água cair.
Das beiras dos telhados,
Cair, sempre cair.

Das beiras dos telhados,
Cair, quase morrer...
Meus olhos apagados,
E cansados de ver.

Meus olhos, afogai-vos
Na vã tristeza ambiente.
Caí e derramai-vos
Como a água morrente.

Il pleure dans mon coeur
Comme il pleut sur la ville.
Verlaine

    My listless eyes,
Watch the water falling.
From the lip of the eaves,
Falling, always falling.

    From the lip of the eaves,
Falling, a kind of dying…
My listless eyes,
Seeing can be so trying.

    Drown yourselves, my eyes,
In the vain sadness of this show.
Fall and shed what you hold back,
Fall as dying waters flow.

Quando se erguerão as seteiras,
Outra vez, do castelo em ruína,
E haverá gritos e bandeiras
Na fria aragem matutina?

Se ouvirá tocar a rebate
Sobre a planície abandonada?
E sairemos ao combate,
De cota e elmo e a longa espada?

Quando iremos, tristes e sérios,
Nas prolixas e vãs contendas,
Soltando juras, impropérios,
Pelas divisas e legendas?

E voltaremos, os antigos,
E puríssimos lidadores,
(Quantos trabalhos e perigos!)
Quase mortos e vencedores?

....

When will the crenels rise again
On castle walls, now in ruins?
And when will shouts and banners there
Traverse the chilly morning air?

Will we hear the alarm resound
High above the abandoned plain?
And set off for the battleground
With helmet, sword, and coat of chain?

When, with melancholia,
Will we depart for vain contentions,
Uttering oaths and imprecations
For legends and insignia?

And when return – the veterans,
The battle-cleansed warriors –
(How much toil, how many dangers!)
The nearly dead and conquerors?

....

E quando, ó Doce Infanta Real,
Nos sorrirás do belveder?
– Magra figura de vitral,
Por quem nós fomos combater...

And when, O Royal Princess, will
You smile upon us from on high?
– A slender figure fit for show
For whom we did to battle go…

a João P. Vasco

O meu coração desce,
Um balão apagado.
Melhor fora que ardesse,
Nas trevas incendiado.

Na bruma fastidienta,
Como um caixão à cova...

Porque antes não rebenta
De dor violenta e nova?

Que apego inda o sustém?
Átono, miserando...

Se o esmagasse o trem
Dum comboio arquejando!

O inane, vil despojo
Da alma egoísta e fraca!

Trouxesse-o o mar de rojo...
Levasse-o na ressaca...

for João P. Vasco

    My heart descends,
A deflating balloon.

    Better yet to have caught fire
And burned within this gloom.

    In the tedious mist
Like a coffin to a grave…

    Why does it not simply burst
From a new and violent pain?

    What attachment still sustains it?
Miserable and inexpressive…

    Better it were crushed instead
By a wheezing locomotive!

    The vile and senseless spoils
Of the weak and selfish soul!

    Would that the sea spouted them forth…
And after swallowed them whole…

I

E eis quanto resta do idílio acabado,
– Primavera que durou um momento...
Como vão longe as manhãs do convento!
– Do alegre conventinho abandonado...

Tudo acabou... Anémonas, hidrângeas,
Silindras, – flores tão nossas amigas!
No claustro agora viçam as ortigas,
Rojam-se cobras pelas velhas lájeas.

Sobre a inscrição do teu nome delido!
– Que os meus olhos mal podem soletrar,
Cansados... E o aroma fenecido

Que se evola do teu nome vulgar!
Enobreceu-o a quietação do olvido.
Ó doce, ingénua, inscrição tumular.

I

    Of the finished idyll this is what remains,
– A spring that lasted for but a moment...
How far off those mornings at the convent!
– At the small, cheerful convent now in ruins...

    Buttercups, hydrangeas, dogwoods –
Such flowers were our friends! But all is gone...
Now in the cloisters the nettles flourish
And snakes slither across weathered flagstone.

    Across the inscription of your worn out name!
– Whose letters my tired eyes can barely
Trace... And the scent of death and decay

    That enwraps your name, as common as day!
Quiet oblivion ennobles its description.
O sweet, innocent, tumular inscription.

II

    Floriram por engano as rosas bravas
No inverno: veio o vento desfolhá-las...
Em que cismas, meu bem? Porque me calas
As vozes com que há pouco me enganavas?

    Castelos doidos! Tão cedo caístes!...
Onde vamos, alheio o pensamento,
De mãos dadas? Teus olhos, que um momento
Perscrutaram nos meus, como vão tristes!

    E sobre nós cai nupcial a neve,
Surda, em triunfo, pétalas, de leve
Juncando o chão, na acrópole de gelos...

    Em redor do teu vulto é como um véu!
Quem as esparze – quanta flor! –, do céu,
Sobre nós dois, sobre os nossos cabelos?

II

The wild roses blossomed mistakenly
In winter: the wind stripped them of their bloom…
What troubles you, my dear? Why silence
The voices you deceived me with so soon?

Absurd castles! So easily you fell!…
Where are we headed, our thoughts unaware,
Hand in hand? Your eyes, which tried to tell
The contents of my own, how sad they appear!

And over us the snow falls nuptial
And deaf, its petals, triumphant in the air,
Blanket this acropolis of ice…

It falls around your figure like a veil!
Who scatters them – endless flowers! – from the sky,
That they might grace our bodies and our hair?

Foi um dia de inúteis agonias,
Dia de sol, inundado de sol.
Fulgiam nuas as espadas frias.
Dia de sol, inundado de sol.

Foi um dia de falsas alegrias:
Dália a esfolhar-se, o seu mole sorriso.
Voltavam os ranchos das romarias.
Dália a esfolhar-se, o seu mole sorriso.

Dia impressível, mais que os outros dias.
Tão lúcido, tão pálido, tão lúcido!
Difuso de teoremas, de teorias.

O dia fútil, mais que os outros dias.
Minuete de discretas ironias.
Tão lúcido, tão pálido, tão lúcido!

It was a day of useless agonies,
A day of sun, a day flooded with sun.
The naked steel of the swords glistened.
A day of sun, a day flooded with sun.

It was a day of hollow gaieties:
Exfoliating dahlia, its bland smile.
The revelers returned from the festivities.
Exfoliating dahlia, its bland smile.

A day more impressible than other days.
So lucid, so pallid, so lucid!
Diffused with theorems and with theories.

A day more futile than other days.
A minuet of discreet ironies.
So lucid, so pallid, so lucid!

Fonógrafo

Vai declamando um cómico defunto.
Uma plateia ri, perdidamente,
Do bom jarreta... E há um odor no ambiente
A cripta e a pó, – do anacrónico assunto.

Muda o registo, eis uma barcarola:
Lírios, lírios, águas do rio, a lua.
Ante o Seu corpo o sonho meu flutua
Sobre um paúl, – extática corola.

Muda outra vez: gorjeios, estribilhos
Dum clarim de oiro – o cheiro de junquilhos,
Vívido e agro! – tocando a alvorada...

Cessou. E, amorosa, a alma das cornetas
Quebra-se agora orvalhada e velada.
Primavera. Manhã. Que eflúvio de violetas!

Phonograph

      Still performing is a dead comedian.
The audience laughs hysterically
At the old fogy… And in the air is a scent
Of death and dust – the anachronic question.

      The register changes, there's a barcarola:
Lilies, lilies, river waters, the moon.
Before His body my dream floats above
These marshlands – ecstatic corolla.

      It changes again: the chirpings, the refrain
Of a golden horn – the scent of jonquils,
Vivid and pungent! – trumpeting the dawn…

      It ceased. And, loving, the soul of the cornets
Came to an end, dewy and obscure.
Spring. Morning. What effusion of violets!

Vida

Choveu! E logo da terra humosa
Irrompe o campo das liliáceas.
Foi bem fecunda, a estação pluviosa!
Que vigor no campo das liliáceas!

Calquem. Recalquem, não o afogam.
Deixem. Não calquem. Que tudo invadam.
Não as extinguem. Porque as degradam?
Para que as calcam? Não as afogam.

Olhem o fogo que anda na serra.
é a queimada... Que lumaréu!
Podem calcá-lo, deitar-lhe terra,
Que não apagam o lumaréu.

Deixem! Não calquem! Deixem arder.
Se aqui o pisam, rebenta além.
– E se arde tudo? – Isso que tem?
Deitam-lhe fogo, é para arder...

Life

    It rained! And from the humid terrain
Burst forth this field of lilies.
It was fecund, the season of rain!
What vigor in this field of lilies!

    Smother it, and again. Still it won't go out.
Leave them be, untrammeled. Let them all invade.
They won't be quelled. Why seek you to degrade?
Why trample them? For still they won't go out.

    Look at the mountains where the fire's aglow.
It's the burn-clearing... What a blaze!
You can stomp it down, bury it below
Piles of earth and not extinguish the blaze.

    Let it be! Don't smother it! Let the fire burn.
If you trample it here, it will burst forth there.
– And if it all catches fire? – What's the care?
Set it all on fire: it is meant to burn...

San Gabriel

No quarto centenário do
descobrimento da Índia

I

Inútil! Calmaria. Já colheram
As velas. As bandeiras sossegaram
Que tão altas nos topes tremularam,
– Gaivotas que a voar desfaleceram.

Pararam de remar! Emudeceram!
(Velhos ritmos que as ondas embalaram).
Que cilada que os ventos nos armaram!
A que foi que tão longe nos trouxeram?

San Gabriel, arcanjo tutelar,
Vem outra vez abençoar o mar.
Vem-nos guiar sobre a planície azul.

Vem-nos levar à conquista final
Da luz, do Bem, doce clarão irreal.
Olhai! Parece o Cruzeiro do Sul!

Saint Gabriel

*No quarto centenário do
descobrimento da Índia*

I

    Useless! A lull. They have gathered up
The sails. The banners have all gone slack
Which once fluttered at the top,
– Seagulls that, in midflight, plummet back.

    They have stopped rowing! They have gone mute!
(Old rhythms that the waves have rocked to sleep)
The winds have laid for us a trap astute!
Why drive this ship so far into the deep?

    Saint Gabriel, archangel and guardian,
Come visit once again to bless the sea.
Come guide us over this blue horizon.

    Come lead us to the final conquest
Of light, of Good, sweet burst of phosphorus.
Look! I swear I can see the Southern Cross!

II

    Vem conduzir as naus, as caravelas,
Outra vez, pela noite, na ardentia,
Avivada das quilhas. Dir-se-ia
Irmos arando em um montão de estrelas.

    Outra vez vamos! Côncavas as velas,
Cuja brancura, rútila de dia,
O luar dulcifica. Feeria
Do luar, não mais deixes de envolvê-las!

    San Gabriel, vem-nos guiar à nebulosa
Que do horizonte vapora, luminosa
E a noite lactescendo, onde, quietas,

    Fulgem as velhas almas namoradas...
– Almas tristes, severas, resignadas,
De guerreiros, de santos, de poetas.

II

    Come, the ships and the caravels you must steer
Once again through the night, amidst the rousing
Phosphorescent glow of the keels. One might say
We are, in a field of stars, plowing our way.

    Once again we are off! Concave the sails
Whose whiteness, scintillating by day,
The moonlight softens. Ravishing moonlight,
From these sails never turn your beams away!

    Saint Gabriel, guide us through the nebulous
Mist rising on the horizon, luminous
And, at night, like spreading milk, where calmly

    Glimmer the ancient, enamoring souls…
– Wistful souls, quiescent and severe,
Of poets, of saints and of warriors.

Viola Chinesa

a Wenceslau de Moraes

    Ao longo da viola morosa
Vai adormecendo a parlenda
Sem que amadornado eu atenda
A lengalenga fastidiosa.

    Sem que o meu coração se prenda,
Enquanto nasal, minuciosa,
Ao longo da viola morosa,
Vai adormecendo a parlenda.

    Mas que cicatriz melindrosa
Há nele que essa viola ofenda
E faz que as asitas distenda
Numa agitação dolorosa?

    Ao longo da viola, morosa...

Chinese Guitar

for Wenceslau de Moraes

     As the measured guitar labors along
The frivolous chatter winds to an end
While I, as drifting to sleep, pay no heed
To what the tedious voices contend.

     Without my heart finding something to tend,
As the measured guitar labors along,
In nasal, meticulous sounds that arise
The frivolous chatter winds to an end.

     But what fragile scar lies buried within
That, with its song, this guitar would offend
And cause my heart to unfurl paltry wings
And beat them to such a harrowing end?

As the measured guitar labors along…

Ao Longe os Barcos de Flores
a Ovídio de Alpoim

Só, incessante, um som de flauta chora,
Viúva, grácil, na escuridão tranquila,
– Perdida voz que de entre as mais se exila,
– Festões de som dissimulando a hora

Na orgia, ao longe, que em clarões cintila
E os lábios, branca, do carmim desflora...
Só, incessante, um som de flauta chora,
Viúva, grácil, na escuridão tranquila.

E a orquestra? E os beijos? Tudo a noite, fora,
Cauta, detém. Só modulada trila
A flauta flébil... Quem há-de remi-la?
Quem sabe a dor que sem razão deplora?

Só, incessante, um som de flauta chora...

Boats of Flowers in the Distance

for Ovídio de Alpoim

 Alone, incessant, rings out a flute's lament,
Widowed, delicate, in the tranquil dark,
– A lost voice, exiled among many others,
– Festoons of sound dissembling the moment

 In the orgy, flashing in the firmament,
Whose white the carmine lips deflowers...
Alone, incessant, rings out a flute's lament,
Widowed, delicate, in the tranquil dark.

 And the orchestra? And the kisses? The night,
Cautious, arrests all. All but the nuanced trill
Of the mournful flute... Who redeem it will?
Who knows the pain it decries in its element?

Alone, incessant, rings out a flute's lament...

Camilo Pessanha at the
Lou Lim Ieoc Garden in Macau.

a João Vasco
(Na ceia da noite de despedida
para uma longa separação)

A boémia não morreu.
Eis-nos com cabelos brancos;
E, todavia, os barrancos
Do seu destino, e do meu,

Se nos quebraram as pernas,
As asas não as partiram.
Em que altos sonhos deliram
As nossas almas eternas.

Depois de tantos baldões,
Devera ter-se ido a fé:
Temos tido pontapé
Das mais caras ilusões...

E não morre a mocidade!
Após enganos, enganos...
Pois só daqui a cem anos
Choraremos de saudade?

to João Vasco
(At the goodbye dinner on the eve
Before a long separation)

 Bohemia is still alive.
Here we are both white of hair;
And, yet, the steep ravines of fate,
Which you and I both share,

 If they've left our legs a wreck,
At least they did not break our wings.
Feverish, our timeless souls
Still dream of lofty things.

 Our faith should long have disappeared
After such misguided fortunes:
We have suffered blows and bruises
From the richest of illusions…

 Youth will never pass away!
After mishaps piled deep…
For only in a hundred years
Will this longing make us weep?

Rosas de Inverno

Corolas, que floristes
Ao sol do inverno, avaro,
Tão glácido e tão claro
Por estas manhãs tristes.

Gloriosa floração,
Surdida, por engano,
No agonizar do ano,
Tão fora da estação!

Sorrindo-vos amigas,
Nos ásperos caminhos,
Aos olhos dos velhinhos,
Às almas das mendigas!

Desse Natal de inválidos
Transmito-vos a bênção,
Com que vos recompensam
Os seus sorrisos pálidos.

Winter Roses

     Corollas who unfolded
To the winter's stingy sun,
So glacial and so clear
On these sad days just begun.

     Gloriously now in bloom,
Sprouting without reason,
In this wretched time of year,
So distant from the season!

     Putting on a friendly smile,
Along the paths that try us all,
To the eyes of aged folks
And to the beggars' souls!

     From that Christmas with the broken
I've a blessing to bestow,
The form they have for giving thanks
For pale smiles as they go.

Em um Retrato

De sob o cômoro quadrangular
Da terra fresca que me há-de inumar,

E depois de já muito ter chovido,
Quando a erva alastrar com o olvido,

Ainda, amigo, o mesmo meu olhar
Há-de ir humilde, atravessando o mar,

Envolver-te de preito enternecido,
Como o de um pobre cão agradecido.

In a Portrait

    Underneath the quadrangular knoll
Of fresh earth that one day will encompass

    My flesh, and after a heavy rainfall,
When the grass spreads out with forgetfulness,

    Still, friend, my regard will make its way
Here, humbly traversing the ocean,

    To surround you with tender devotion,
Like the eyes of a poor, beholden stray.

Desce enfim sobre o meu coração
O olvido. Irrevocável. Absoluto.
Envolve-o grave como um véu de luto.
Podes, corpo, ir dormir no teu caixão.

A fronte já sem rugas, distendidas
As feições, na imortal serenidade,
Dorme enfim sem desejo e sem saudade
Das coisas não logradas ou perdidas.

O barro que em quimera modelaste
Quebrou-se-te nas mãos, Viça uma flor,
Pões-lhe o dedo, ei-la murcha sobre a haste...

Ias andar, sempre fugia o chão,
Até que desvairavas, do terror,
Corria-te um suor, de inquietação...

It descends at last to cover my heart,
Oblivion. Absolute. Final.
It surrounds my heart gravely like a veil.
Now, body, you may sleep within your pall.

Your brow unwrinkled, your features spreading
Out into immortal serenity,
Sleep at last without desire or longing
For things departed or unachieved.

The clay you molded into a chimera
Came apart in your hands. The vibrant flower
You newly touched wilted on the stem…

With each step you took the ground beneath you fled,
Until you grew demented from the terror.
Drops of sweat, in angst, from your body bled…

Porque o melhor, enfim,
É não ouvir nem ver…
Passarem sobre mim
E nada me doer!

– Sorrindo interiormente,
Co'as pálpebras cerradas,
Às águas da torrente
Já tão longe passadas. –

Rixas, tumultos, lutas,
Não me fazerem dano…
Alheio às vãs labutas,
Às estações do ano.

Passar o estio, o outono,
A poda, a cava , e a redra,
E eu dormindo um sono
D ebaixo duma pedra.

Melhor até se o acaso
O leito me reserva
No prado extenso e raso
Apenas sob a erva

Because the best, alas,
Is neither to see nor hear...
When over me they pass
Never to shed a tear!

– With a smile inwardly cast,
And eyelids firmly shut,
At the torrents of water
That have long since passed. –

Quarrels, scuffles, fights
Leave me no worse for wear...
Indifferent to vain toils,
Or the seasons of the year.

Summer and autumn have moved on,
Pruning, digging, weeding done,
And I am in a dream-filled dream
Stretched out beneath a stone.

Better even if it be
The bed that is reserved for me
In pasture low and vast
Is merely covered by the grass

Que Abril copioso ensope...
E, esbelto, a intervalos
Fustigue-me o galope
De bandos de cavalos,

Ou no serrano mato,
A brigas tão propício,
Onde o viver ingrato
Dispõe ao sacrifício

Das vidas, mortes duras
Ruam pelas quebradas,
Com choques de armaduras
E tinidos de espadas...

Ou sob o piso, até,
Infame e vil da rua,
Onde a torva ralé
Irrompe, tumultua,

Se estorce, vocifera,
Selvagem nos conflitos,
Com ímpetos de fera
Nos olhos, saltos, gritos...

Roubos, assassinatos!
Horas jamais tranquilas,
Em brutos pugilatos
Fracturam-se as maxilas...

That April inundates…
And in noble intervals
The galloping of wild herds
My spirit castigates.

Or in the thick of mountain bush
Where fights are quick to break
And having little to suffice
Disposes to the sacrifice

Of lives, exacting deaths
Circulate throughout the glades
To the crash of armor
And the clang of warring blades…

Or even under floorboards,
Vile and wretched of the street,
Where the grim and vulgar hoards
Erupt in tumultuous play.

They mill about, vociferous,
Savage in their rivalries,
With a beast-like impetus
In their gestures, shouts, and eyes…

Robberies and killings!
No peace the hour knows
In brutal acts of combat
Jaws are shattered under blows…

E eu sob a terra firme,
Compacta, recalcada,
Muito quietinho. A rir-me
De não me doer nada.

And I beneath the earthen floor,
Compact and firmly pressed,
Lie very still but still can laugh
Since nothing hurts me any more.

Rufando apressado,
E bamboleado,
Boné posto ao lado,

　　Garboso, o tambor
Avança em redor
Do campo de amor...

　　Com força, soldado!
A passo dobrado!
Bem bamboleado!

　　Amor's te bafejem.
Que as moças te beijem.
Que os moços te invejem.

　　Mas ai, ó soldado!
Ó triste alienado!
Por mais exaltado

　　Que o toque reclame,
Ninguém que te chame...
Ninguém que te ame...

    Hurriedly, with lively roll,
And swaying side to side,
Cap crookedly in place,

    The drum, dignified,
Advances to embrace
The field of love...

    With effort, soldier!
Double your pace!
Swagger on with style and grace!

    May loves tender their caress.
May lasses long for your kiss.
May lads envy your success.

    Alas, soldier, the distress!
How dejected and alone!
For as loudly as the chime

    Does within the air resound,
No one there to call your name...
None to love you can be found...

Tatuagens complicadas do meu peito!
– Troféus, emblemas, dois leões alados...
Mais, entre corações engrinaldados,
Um enorme, soberbo, amor-perfeito.

E o meu brasão... Tem de oiro, num quartel
Vermelho, um lis. Tem no outro uma donzela,
Em campo azul, de prata o corpo, - aquela
Que é no meu braço como um broquel.

Timbre: rompente, a megalomania.
Divisa: um ai, – que insiste noite e dia
Lembrando ruínas, sepulturas rasas.

Entre castelos, serpes batalhantes,
E águias de negro, desfraldando as asas,
Que realça de oiro um colar de besantes.

  Intricate tattoos displayed upon my chest!
– Trophies, emblems, two lions with wings…
And, among hearts with wreaths encircling,
A giant, splendid love-in-idleness.

  And my crest… In gold, in one red quarter,
Is a fleur-de-lis; in another a maiden,
her body in silver against a blue field,
the maiden I wear on my arm like a shield.

  Tone: insolent, a boastful haughtiness…
Motto: a lament – which night and day pervades,
Recalling ruins and thoughts of shallow graves.

  Among castles, battling serpents
And eagles in black, unfurling their wings,
Above the gleaming gold of the bezants.

Branco e Vermelho

    A dor, forte e imprevista,
Ferindo-me, imprevista,
De branca e de imprevista
Foi um deslumbramento,
Que me endoidou a vista,
Fez-me perder a vista,
Fez-me fugir a vista,
Num doce esvaimento.

    Como um deserto imenso,
Branco deserto imenso,
Resplandecente e imenso,
Fez-se em redor de mim.
Todo o meu ser, suspenso,
Não sinto já, não penso,
Pairo na luz, suspenso...
Que delícia sem fim!

White and Red

    The pain, sharp and unforeseen,
Wounding me, unforeseen,
With a whiteness unforeseen
Was a moment of wonder
That befuddled seeing,
Made me lose sight,
Made me vanish from sight,
And gently pulled me under.

    Like a desert immense,
A desert white and immense,
Dazzling and immense,
It sprang up to surround.
All of my being suspended,
Nothing felt or apprehended,
I hang in the light, suspended…
What delight without bound!

Na inundação da luz
Banhando os céus a flux,
No êxtase da luz,
Vejo passar, desfila
(Seus pobres corpos nus
Que a distância reduz,
Amesquinha e reduz
No fundo da pupila)

Na areia imensa e plana
Ao longe a caravana
Sem fim, a caravana
Na linha do horizonte
Da enorme dor humana,
Da insigne dor humana...
A inútil dor humana!
Marcha, curvada a fronte.

Até o chão, curvados,
Exaustos e curvados,
Vão um a um, curvados,
Os seus magros perfis;
Escravos condenados,
No poente recortados,
Em negro recortados,
Magros, mesquinhos, vis.

    In the flood of light
That bathes the skies with its flux
In the ecstasy of light
I watch the pageant passing by
(Their bodies indigent and bare
That distance works to minimize,
To humble and to minimize,
In the recess of the eye)

    On the sand immense and flat,
Far away the caravan
Without end, the caravan
Far off on the horizon
Of the vast human suffering,
Of the august human suffering…
The useless human suffering!
Heads bowed, they still march on.

    To the ground, heads bowed,
Exhausted and bowed,
One by one, heads bowed,
Their slim shapes in profile;
Convicted slaves,
With the setting sun in back,
Slender cutouts all in black,
Meager, mean and vile.

A cada golpe tremem
Os que de medo tremem,
E as pálpebras me tremem
Quando o açoite vibra.
Estala! e apenas gemem,
Palidamente gemem,
A cada golpe gemem,
Que os desequilibra.

Sob o açoite caem,
A cada golpe caem,
Erguem-se logo. Caem,
Soergue-os o terror...
Até que enfim desmaiem,
Por uma vez desmaiem!
Ei-los que enfim se esvaem,
Vencida, enfim, a dor...

E ali fiquem serenos,
De costas e serenos.
Beije-os a luz, serenos,
Nas amplas frontes calmas.
Ó céus claros e amenos,
Doces jardins amenos,
Onde se sofre menos,
Onde dormem as almas!

With every strike they tremble,
Those that from fear tremble,
And my eyelids tremble
When the whip dances.
Snaps! And they but grumble,
Pallidly grumble,
With each strike grumble,
As it makes them stumble.

　　Beneath the whip they fall,
With each strike they fall,
And rise at once. They fall,
Then bristle with terror…
Until at last they faint,
In the end they faint!
Watch them finally dissipate,
The pain at last their victor…

　　And there they sit, serene,
Backs turned and serene…
Kissed by the light, serene,
On their calm and ample faces.
Oh, skies, sunny and fair,
Gardens gentle and fair,
The places pain is lessened,
And their souls' resting places!

A dor, deserto imenso,
Branco deserto imenso,
Resplandecente e imenso,
Foi um deslumbramento.
Todo o meu ser suspenso,
Não sinto já, não penso,
Pairo na luz, suspenso
Num doce esvaimento.

Ó morte, vem depressa,
Acorda, vem depressa,
Acode-me depressa,
Vem-me enxugar o suor,
Que o estertor começa.
É cumprir a promessa.
Já o sonho começa...
Tudo vermelho em flor...

The pain, a desert immense,
A desert white and immense,
Dazzling and immense,
It was a moment of wonder.
All of my being suspended,
Nothing felt or apprehended,
I hang in the light, suspended,
And am gently pulled under.

Oh, Death, come quickly,
Wake up, come quickly,
Respond to me quickly,
Wipe the droplets from my head.
For the rattle has begun.
The promise kept by everyone.
The dream has already begun…
All is blossoming in red…

Ó cores virtuais que jazeis subterrâneas,
– Fulgurações azuis, vermelhos de hemoptise,
Represados clarões, cromáticas vesânias –,
No limbo onde esperais a luz que vos baptize,

As pálpebras cerrai, ansiosas não veleis.

Abortos que pendeis as frontes cor de cidra,
Tão graves de cismar, nos bocais dos museus,
E escutando o correr da água na clepsydra,
Vagamente sorris, resignados e ateus,

Cessai de cogitar, o abismo não sondeis.

Gemebundo arrulhar dos sonhos não sonhados,
Que toda a noite errais, doces almas penando,
E as asas lacerais na aresta dos telhados,
E no vento expirais em um queixume brando,

Adormecei. Não suspireis. Não respireis.

O virtual colors that lie subterranean,
– Fulgurating blues and reds hemoptysized,
Muffled flashes, dementia chromatized –,
In the limbo where you await the baptismal light,

Close your eyelids, grant your anxious vigil reprieve.

Fetuses suspended with brows tinged the color of sidra,
So vexing to behold, in the jars of the museum,
And hearing the water as it runs through the clepsydra,
You smile vaguely, atheist and overcome,

Cease to ponder, do not fathom the abyss.

Melancholy cooing of the dreams undreamt,
Which all night float by, sweet suffering souls,
Whose wings get torn on the rooftop eaves,
And who exhale in the wind a quiet dissent,

Fall asleep. Do not murmur. Do not breathe.

Unfinished Poems, Two Satirical Sonnets and Fragments Recalled from Memory by Others

UNFINISHED POEMS, TWO SATIRICAL SONNETS AND FRAGMENTS RECALLED FROM MEMORY BY OTHERS

The verses of the first section were collected by one of the first publishers of *Clepsydra* and grouped together to form a poem. The texts, handwritten in pencil by Camilo Pessanha in a notebook, present a significant number of obstacles to their reading and, to all indications, were never considered finished by the poet himself. This is what we can infer from an analysis of the available documents: Pessanha never referred to these lines in any document; he never attributed a date to indicate the conclusion of a first version (a practice he followed even when significantly altering the text subsequently); and he never added the word "clean" to the manuscript, as he had done with so many other poems, including the significant smudging of the corrections to the poem "Life" ("Vida").

The satirical sonnets, which the poet claims to be "imitations" of a rival poet's style, were included in a letter by Pessanha dated 8 October 1916 and sent from Macau to Henrique Trindade Coelho. They were thus written after his last visit to Portugal. The sonnets were never published in Pessanha's lifetime, nor was any version of them recorded in the notebook in which he collected his work.

There is no manuscript version of the fragments: the first of these – belonging to a poem called "Ode to the earth" ("Ode à terra"), now lost – was reconstructed from memory by Carlos Amaro; the second – which was part of a sonnet composed in Lisbon in 1916 and has also been lost – was transcribed by João de Castro Osório, who would have heard it recited by Camilo Pessanha.

Unfinished Poems

Enfim, levantou ferro.
Com os lenços adeus, vai partir o navio.
Longe das pedras más do meu desterro,
Ondas do azul oceano, submergi-o.

Que eu, desde a partida,
Não sei onde vou.
Roteiro da vida,
Quem é que o traçou?

Nalguma rocha ignota
Se vai despedaçar, com violento fragor...
Mareante, deixa as cartas da derrota.
Maquinista, dá mais força no vapor.

Nem sei de onde venho,
Que azar me fadou?
Das mágoas que tenho,
Os ais porque os dou...

At last the anchor was raised.
With waving handkerchiefs, the ship sets sail.
Far from the cursed stones of my exile,
Waves of the blue ocean, sweep it under.

For I, since making to depart,
Have lost the journey's end.
O course of life,
Who was it that prepared your chart?

On some as yet uncertain rock
It will break up with violent roar…
Sailor, discard those charts of defeat.
Machinist, apply extra vapor.

Unsure of where I come from,
Why misfortune was foretold?
Or why I seem to languish in
These heartaches that I hold…

    Ou siga, maldito,
Co'a bandeira amarela...
....
Pomares, chalés, mercados, cidades...

    A olhar da amurada,
Que triste que estou!
Miragens do nada,
Dizei-me quem sou...

    Carry on, accursed one,
With the yellow flag...
....
Orchards, chalets, markets, cities...

    Gazing out from the ship's railing,
How wretched I am!
Mirages of nothing,
Tell me who I am...

Cristalizações salinas,
Mirrai na areia o plasma vivaz,
Não se desenvolvam as ptomaínas.
Que adocicado! Que obsessão de cheiro!
Putrescina! – Flor de lilás!
Cadaverina! – Branca flor do espinheiro!

    Saline crystallizations,
Desiccate the teeming plasma on the sand,
Before the ptomaines proliferate.
How saccharine! What obsession of perfume!
Putrescine! – The lilacs in blossom
Cadaverine! – White hawthorn flower in bloom!

Só o meu crânio fique
Rolando insepulto no areal
Ao abandono e ao acaso do simum…
Que o sol e o sal o purifique

My skull alone does yet reside
Lolling unburied on this stretch of sand.
Abandoned to the fortune of the Simoom…
That it might, by sun and salt, be purified.

Nesgas agudas do areal
E gaivotas que voais em redor do navio,
Tomai o meu cérebro mole,
– Esmeralda viva do Canal
E desertos inundados de sol! –
Meu pobre cérebro inconsequente e doentio!

No qual uma rede se desenha,
Complicada de sofrimentos irregulares
– Águas que filtrais na areia! –
Antes que o crepúsculo venha,
O crepúsculo e as larvas tumulares,
A impureza inútil dissolvei-a.

Que o sol sem mancha, o cristal sereno,
Volatilize ao seu doce calor
A fria e exangue liquescência.
Um hálito! Não embaciará de veneno
Indecisa, incolor
Do azul o brilho e a viva transparência
Recortes vivos das areias,
Tomai meu corpo e abride-lhe as veias.
O meu sangue {?tomai-o}
Difundi-o sob o rútilo sol,
Na areia branca como em um lençol,
– Ao sol triunfante, sob o qual desmaio.

Jagged fingers of the sands
And seagulls circling the vessel,
The soft putty of my brain become,
– The bright emerald of the channel
And deserts flooded with rays of the sun! –
My poor brain, sick and inconsequential!

In which a net begins to be drawn,
An intricate net of uneven pain
– What waters you purify in the sand! –
Before at last the twilight closes in,
The twilight and the larvae of the grave,
The useless impurity dissolve.

That the spotless sun, the serene crystal,
Might, in its sweet warmth, render volatile
The cold and bloodless liquid form.
A breath! It will not cloud with poison,
This lack of color and decision,
The bright and spry transparency of blue
The living contours of the sands,
Take my body and open up its veins.
Take my blood and let it issue forth,
Pour it out beneath a glimmering sun
On the white sand as if upon a linen.
– To the triumphant sun, beneath which I succumb.

Two Satirical Sonnets

Camilo Pessanha | Two Satirical Sonnets

I (ou II)
A Miragem

    Parei a cogitar. No meu cabelo
Torvelinhava um vento de oração...
– Qual a acha que ardeu, feita carvão,
– A água que esfriou, tornada gelo.

    Ajoelhei. O meu peito era um vulcão.
No céu lacrimejava o Sete-Estrelo...
E o seu fino perfil pude inda vê-lo,
Num halo de pudor e devoção.

    Mas no meu coração, ardente lava,
Uma nuvem errática poisava,
E que ao longe obumbrou saudosas fráguas;

    Hóstia santa de luz, desfeita em chuva,
Qual beguina do Amor, de Deus viúva,
Num rosário a rezar, vertendo águas.

I (or II)
The Mirage

     I stopped to deliberate. In my hair
Was swirling a whirlwind of prayer…
– What timber had caught fire and turned to coal,
– The water that grew cold and turned to ice.

     I knelt. A volcano was my chest.
In the sky Pleiades had begun to tear…
And its slender profile I still could glimpse
In a halo of humble deference.

     But in the fiery lava of my chest
An erratic cloud had come to rest
And cast its shadow over wistful cliffs;

     Sacred host of light, to rain turned of late,
A beguine of Love, God's widowed bride,
Praying on a rosary amidst the spate.

II (ou I)
Transfiguração

    Estrela do Pastor, – sol que me escuda!
Mais te afastas de mim, mais eu te vejo.
No instante em que me deste aquele beijo,
A charneca ajoelhou, divina e muda.

    Febricito arco-íris de desejo
(Senhora do Amparo nos acuda)...
Urros dos vagalhões, hoje caluda.
O Requiem salmodiai, vozes do brejo.

    Mulher forte, remiu-me a tua prece:
Penitente, pagão, bem lusitano,
Ergo os braços ao céu quando anoitece.

    Judas divaga, em 'spiras de pecado...
Eis-me o Verbo de Deus, sacramentado
No rebuço dum capote alentejano.

II (or I)
Transfiguration

    Evening Star – sun that is my shield!
The more you stray, the more of you I see.
The moment you your kiss bestowed on me,
The heath knelt down, divine and mute.

    I tremble with a rainbow of desire
(Lady of the Forsaken, give us aid)…
Waves of roaring that today are still.
Chant, psalmodic voices of the mire.

    Strong woman, your prayers did heed my calls:
Penitent, Pagan, Lusitano true,
I raise my arms to Heaven when night falls.

    Judas meanders in spirals of sin…
Here I stand, the Word God spoke,
Sanctified in Alentejan cloak.

Fragments Recalled from Memory by Others

Ó Terra doce e boa,
Ó minha amante gorda!
Desculpa-me, perdoa
Se te esqueci, embora...

Ó doce Esposa de Indra
Sobre os dois pés sentada!

O Terra, sweet and good,
O my corpulent lover!
Pardon me, I wish you would,
If I've neglected you, although…

Wife of Indra – oh, how sweet –
Sitting there upon both feet!

Um fio a desdobar, que não termina,
De grinaldas de rosas de toucar.

A thread unfolding, never ending,
Of garlands of roses embellishing.

On The Poetry of Camilo Pessanha, in Portuguese

Franchetti, Paulo. 1995. "Introdução". In *Clepsydra*. Lisboa: Relógio D'Água Editores.

Franchetti, Paulo. 2001. *Nostalgia, exílio e melancolia — leituras de Camilo Pessanha*. São Paulo: Editora da Universidade de São Paulo.

Franchetti, Paulo. 2008. *O essencial sobre Camilo Pessanha*. Lisboa: Imprensa Nacional/Casa da Moeda.

Gomes, Álvaro Cardoso.1977. *A metáfora cósmica em Camilo Pessanha*. São Paulo: Universidade de São Paulo.

Lemos, Esther de. 1956. *A Clepsidra de Camilo Pessanha*. Porto: Livraria Tavares Martins.

Lopes, Óscar. 1969. "Pessanha, o quebrar dos espelhos". In *Ler e depois*. Porto: Inova.

Lopes, Óscar. 1987. "Camilo Pessanha". In: *Entre Fialho e Nemésio — Estudos de Literatura Portuguesa Contemporânea*, v. I. Lisboa: Imprensa Nacional/Casa da Moeda.

Miguel, António Dias. 1956. *Camilo Pessanha — Elementos para o estudo da sua biografia e da sua obra*. Lisboa: Ocidente.

Monteiro, Maria Ofélia Paiva. 1969. "O universo poético de Camilo Pessanha". Coimbra: Separata do Arquivo Coimbrão.

Oliveira, António Falcão de. 1979. *O simbolismo de Camilo Pessanha*. Lisboa: Ática.

Pires, Daniel. 2005. *A imagem e o verbo — fotobiografia de Camilo Pessanha*. Macau: Instituto Cultura do Governo da R.A.E. de Macau/Instituto do Oriente.

Pires, Daniel, ed.. 1990. "Homenagem a Camilo Pessanha". Macau: Instituto Português do Oriente/Instituto Cultural de Macau.

Pires, Daniel, ed.. 1992. *Camilo Pessanha: prosador e tradutor*. Macau: Instituto Português do Oriente/Instituto Cultural de Macau.

Rubim, Gustavo. 1993. *Experiência da alucinação — Camilo Pessanha e a questão da poesia*. Lisboa: Editorial Caminho.

Simões, João Gaspar. 1967. *Camilo Pessanha*. Lisboa: Arcádia.

Spaggiari, Barbara. 1982. *O Simbolismo na obra de Camilo Pessanha*. Lisboa: ICALP.

On The Poetry of Camilo Pessanha, in English

Cohen, Rip. "Footsteps in the Nineteenth Century Sand: Camilo Pessanha and Erotic Poetics". Colóquio/Letras (2008), http://coloquio.gulbenkian.pt/docs/Footsteps%20 in%20the%20nineteenth%20century%20sand.pdf

Portuguese Poetry Translated into English

Almeida, Onésimo Teotónio, ed., and George Monteiro, trans. 1983. *The Sea Within: A Selection of Azorean Poems*. Providence, RI: Gávea-Brown.

Andrade, Eugénio de, and Alexis Levitin, trans. 1996. *The Shadow's Weight*. Providence, RI: Gávea-Brown.

Botto, António, and Fernando Pessoa, trans. 2010. *The Songs of António Botto*, edited by Josiah Blackmore. Minneapolis, MN: University of Minnesota Press.

Camões, Luís de, and Keith Bosley, trans. 1990. *Epic & Lyric*. Edited by L. C. Taylor. Manchester: Carcanet Press, in association with the Calouste Gulbenkian Foundation.

Camões, Luís de, and Landeg White, trans. 1997. *The Lusiads*. Oxford: Oxford University Press.

Camões, Luís de, and Landeg White, trans. 2008. *The Collected Lyric Poems of Luís de Camões*. Princeton, NJ: Princeton University Press.

Camões, Luís de, and Richard Zenith, trans. 2009. *Sonnets and Other Poems*. Dartmouth, MA: University of Massachusetts.

Camões, Luís de, and William Baer, trans. 2005. *Selected Sonnets*. Chicago, IL: University of Chicago Press.

Camões, Luís de, and William C. Atkinson, trans. 1973. *The Lusiads*. Harmondsworth, Middlesex: Penguin Books.

D'Evelin, Martin, trans., and Austen Hyde, trans. 2015. *Lisbon Poets - Camões, Cesário, Sá-Carneiro, Florbela, Pessoa*. Lisbon: Lisbon Poets & Co.

Longland, Jean R., trans. 1966. *Selections from Contemporary Portuguese Poetry: A Bilingual Selection*. New York: Harvey House.

Macedo, Helder, and Ernesto Manuel de Melo e Castro, eds. 1978. *Contemporary Portuguese Poetry: An Anthology in English*. Manchester: Carcanet New Press.

Pessoa, Fernando, and David Butler, trans. 2004. *Selected Poems*. Dublin: Dedalus.

Pessoa, Fernando, and George Monteiro, trans. 1988. *Self-Analysis and Thirty Other Poems*. Lisbon: Calouste Gulbenkian Foundation.

Pessoa, Fernando, and Jonathan Griffin, trans. 2007. *Message; Mensagem*. Exeter: Shearsman Books & Menard Press.

Pessoa, Fernando, and Richard Zenith, trans. 1998. *Fernando Pessoa & Co.: Selected Poems*. New York: Grove Press.

Pessoa, Fernando, and Richard Zenith, trans. 2006. *A Little Larger Than the Entire Universe: Selected Poems*. New York: Penguin Books.

Pessoa, Fernando, and Richard Zenith, trans. 2008. *Forever Someone Else: Selected Poems*. Lisboa: Assírio & Alvim.

Quental, Antero de, and Edgar Prestage, trans. 1894. *Anthero de Quental: Sixty-Four Sonnets Englished by Edgar Prestage*. London: D. Nutt.

Quental, Antero de, and S. Griswold Morley, trans. 1973. *Sonnets and Poems of Anthero de Quental*. Westport, CT: Greenwood Press.

Sena, Jorge de, and George Monteiro, trans. 1980. *In Crete, with the Minotaur, and Other Poems*. Providence, RI: Gávea-Brown.

Torga, Miguel, and George Monteiro, trans. 2004. *Iberian Poems*. Providence, RI: Gávea-Brown

Verde, Cesário, and Austen Hyde, trans. 2016. *The Book of Cesário Verde & other poems*. Lisbon: Lisbon Poets & Co.

Verde, Cesário, and Richard Zenith, trans. 2011. *The Feeling of a Westerner*. Dartmouth, MA: University of Massachusetts.

Zenith, Richard, trans. 1999. *Portuguese Poetry after Pessoa*. Lisboa: Contexto.

Zenith, Richard, trans., and Alexis Levitin, trans. 2015. *28 Portuguese Poets: A Bilingual Anthology*, edited by Richard Zenith. Dublin: Dedalus.

On Portuguese Poetry and Literature

Earle, Thomas F. 1980. *Theme and Image in the Poetry of Sá de Miranda*. Oxford: Oxford University Press.

Earle, Thomas F. 1988. *The Muse Reborn: The Poetry of António Ferreira*. Oxford: Clarendon Press.

Kotowicz, Zbigniew. 2008. *Fernando Pessoa: Voices of a Nomadic Soul*. Exeter: Shearsman Books.

Macedo, Helder, ed. 1992. *Studies in Portuguese Literature and History in honour of Luís de Sousa Rebelo*. London: Tamesis Books.

Monteiro, George, ed. 1982. *The Man Who Never Was: Essays on Fernando Pessoa*. Providence, RI: Gávea-Brown.

Monteiro, George. 1996. *The Presence of Camões: Influences on the Literature of England, America, and Southern Africa*. Lexington, KY: University Press of Kentucky.

Monteiro, George. 1998. *The Presence of Pessoa: English, American, and Southern African Literary Responses*. Lexington, KY: University Press of Kentucky.

Monteiro, George. 2000. *Fernando Pessoa and Nineteenth-Century Anglo-American Literature*. Lexington, KY: University Press of Kentucky.

Parkinson, Stephen, Cláudia Pazos Alonso, and Thomas F. Earle, eds. 2009. *A Companion to Portuguese Literature*. Woodbridge: Tamesis.

Sadlier, Darlene J. 1998. *An Introduction to Fernando Pessoa: Modernism and the Paradoxes of Authorship*. Gainesville: University Press of Florida.

Tamen, Miguel, and Helena Carvalhão Buescu, eds. 1999. *A Revisionary History of Portuguese Literature*. New York: Garland Pub.

Vieira, Nelson H., ed. 1983. *Roads to Today's Portugal: Essays on Contemporary Portuguese Literature, Art and Culture*. Providence, RI: Gávea-Brown.